Music for Film and Game Soundtracks with FL Studio

Learn music production, compose orchestral music, and launch your music career

Joshua Au-Yeung

BIRMINGHAM—MUMBAI

Music for Film and Game Soundtracks with FL Studio

Copyright © 2022 Packt Publishing

Group Product Manager: Rohit Rajkumar
Publishing Product Manager: Kaustubh Manglurkar
Senior Editor: Hayden Edwards
Content Development Editor: Abhishek Jadhav
Technical Editor: Shubham Sharma
Copy Editor: Safis Editing
Project Coordinator: Rashika Ba
Proofreader: Safis Editing
Indexer: Manju Arasan
Production Designer: Shyam Sundar Korumilli
Marketing Coordinator: Elizabeth Varghese

First published: April 2022

Production reference: 4090922

Published by Packt Publishing Ltd.
Livery Place
35 Livery Street
Birmingham
B3 2PB, UK.

ISBN 978-1-80323-329-1

www.packt.com

To my parents—my mother, for her devotion, love, and care, and my father, for his boundless curiosity, support, and determination.

To my friends—Sasha, for her encouragement, support, and always making me feel listened to and appreciated, and Jagdeep, Pavel, and Ryan, for making me laugh.

– Joshua Au-Yeung

Contributors

About the author

Joshua Au-Yeung (professionally known as Chester Sky) is a music producer, composer, director, and software developer. He's published 10+ music albums, directed and composed for films, created board games and dozens of art pieces, and hosts a podcast. He's an instructor of online courses, including best-selling courses on music production and composing for films and video games. His previous book, *The Music Producer's Ultimate Guide to FL Studio 20*, reached #1 on Amazon in the Digital Audio Production category.

To learn more, visit `https://www.chestersky.com/`.

About the reviewer

Shreevathsa PK started his music journey at the age of 5. He started attending Carnatic classical music singing classes at a very young age. Shreevathsa completed juniors with 95% in the Carnatic classical music examination and started learning piano on his own at the age of 13, referring to many sources on the internet. He was fascinated by the variety of western music and how much impact it has on one's personal life.

At the age of 15, he started composing music with the help of DAWs, such as FL Studio Logic Pro. Shreevathsa composes music of various genres. In his free time, he loves to listen to a wide variety of music varying from classical music to electronic dance music to music from various countries, such as Japan, China, Korea, and the Middle East.

Shreevathsa has composed music for short films and collaborated with a few YouTubers, helping with background music for their YouTube channels. He also has his own channels where he posts compositions. Shreevathsa is also an electronics engineer working at an MNC. He dedicates a few hours to music every day, despite working in a busy industry.

Table of Contents

Preface

Part 1: The Business of Composing for Clients

1

The Business of Composing for Clients

Landing your first composing gig	4
How to establish yourself as a professional	5
How to network	6
What if I don't already have a portfolio of music?	7
Preparing for meeting clients	10
Planning a music score	11
The music design document	12
Composing for films	12
Composing for video games	12
Gathering soundtrack requirements for the design document	13
Watching the film with the client	14
Creating a Soundtrack Planner	15
Researching music ideas for the project	18

Collaborating with others	19
Problems with collaborating	19
Version control with Splice	20
Advice for avoiding rookie mistakes	23
Get the project in writing	24
Ask for feedback	25
The day-to-day tasks of composing	26
How to collect music royalties	27
Summary	30

Part 2: Composing Tools and Techniques

2

Navigating Through the Key Features of FL Studio

What is FL Studio?	34	The Mixer	50
Get FL Studio	34	The Browser	54
FL Studio core tools	35	Recording audio	56
The Channel rack	38	Exporting music	59
Using the Piano roll	41	Summary	63
The Playlist	45		

3

Designing Music with Themes, Leitmotifs, and Scales

Toolkit of the composer	66	What are scales?	74
Themes, motifs, and leitmotifs	67	Why are scales important for composing and how do you use scales to compose?	74
Motif	67		
Theme	67		
Leitmotif	68	Understanding modes	79
How to use motifs, themes, and leitmotifs	68	How to use modes	82
Understanding scales	70	Understanding sharps and flats	90
What is 12-tone equal temperament frequency (Hz)?	73	Using the Circle of Fifths chord wheel	92
Why does Western music use 12 notes?	74	Summary	96

4

Orchestral MIDI Composing

Why learn orchestral composing?	98	What makes instrument plugins sound real?	102
Recommended orchestral tool plugins	98	Using velocity	103
Recommended paid instrument plugins	101	Using articulations	109
		Using expression	111

Orchestral MIDI programming 118

Composing for string instruments 119

Tips for composing orchestral chord progressions 122

Tips for making sampled instruments sound realistic 126

Considerations for mixing orchestral compositions 128

Summary 131

Part 3: Designing Music for Films and Video Games

5

Creating Sheet Music with MuseScore, Scoring with Fruity Video Player, and Diegetic Music

Creating sheet music in MuseScore from an FL Studio project 136

Syncing music to visuals using Fruity Video Player 143

Setting markers 147

Setting time signatures 150

Diegetic music (The Art of Foley) and sound effects 153

Sound effect examples 154

Recommended sound effect plugins 155

Sound effect libraries 159

Summary 160

6

Influencing Mood with Music and Designing Emotional Music

Composing spooky music 162

What is fear? 162

Designing a jump scare 164

Designing creepy music 168

Creepy and scary music note combinations 176

Composing music for specific moods 183

Composing happy music 184

Composing sad music 185

Composing romantic music 187

Creating tension/composing epic music for trailers 188

Summary 190

7

Creating Interactive Music for Video Games with Wwise

What is interactive music?	192	Understanding vertical remixing	207
Introduction to Wwise	194	Implementing vertical remixing in Wwise	207
Understanding horizontal re-sequencing	203	Creating music for vertical remixing in FL Studio	215
Implementing horizontal re-sequencing in Wwise	204	Summary	220

8

Soundtrack Composing Templates

Overcoming writer's block	224	Next steps	232
Soundtrack composing templates	227	More from the author	233
Soundtrack requirements checklist	227	Video courses	234
Composing music checklist	229	Social accounts	234
Mixing music checklist	230		
Summary	231	Further reading	235
Share your music	232	Conclusion	235
		A few final thoughts	235

Index

Other Books You May Enjoy

Preface

Think about your favorite movie or video game. Each of these had a soundtrack created for them, a score carefully designed to set the tone and emotional experience. Whenever you sense the intensity of a film or game changing, this is largely due to how the music makes you feel.

Now imagine you were the person that created that music? How exciting it must have felt when composing? The fun, adrenaline rush, and sense of achievement. Masterfully crafting music to take listeners on an adventure. Music that tugs at their heartstrings, bringing them to the edge of their seats in anticipation, filling their thoughts with joy or sorrow. You can be that musician. You can dream up music and bring it to life to entertain listeners around the world.

If you're reading this book, it means that you want to create music that makes your audience feel something. You want to curate an experience for your listener. Perhaps you have a film or a video game you want to cultivate music for. Perhaps you need music for a live event and are wondering how to design the music to fit the setting. Or perhaps you're an aspiring musician and want to make more impactful songs. If any of these apply to you, you're in the right place. This book will take you on a journey from the ground up to build emotional soundtracks.

There's a huge array of topics that can be included in the composition of music. It's very easy to veer off in an interesting direction yet have very little to show for it. This book is designed to help cut through all the time-wasting mumbo jumbo and get right to the practical stuff you can use.

Who this book is for

This book is for musicians, aspiring composers, music producers, and music students. Although we do explore a little theory, this book is more focused on the practical application of software tools and techniques. It's geared toward the aspiring professional who wants to know about the tools and techniques in the craft. This book assumes no pre-existing skills or experience prior to reading.

If your goal is to compose music just for fun, this book will provide you with a practical music foundation to help improve your music compositions. You'll be supplied with music theory to understand the fundamentals of composing songs. You'll learn how to compose for orchestral instruments and make orchestral arrangements. You'll learn how to do this with software without needing to know how to play any actual instruments prior to reading (although some familiarity with the piano will prove helpful). You'll learn how to improve your songs and tailor them to fit specific emotions and moods. You'll also find tips for coming up with music ideas to avoid writer's block.

If you want to get paid for making music, this book will set you up with the tools and techniques to embark on a career as a music consultant. If you want to compose music at a more serious level, rather than just as a hobby, you need to think about how to compose efficiently to a deadline. Once you get an assignment, you need to focus on the important tasks so you can deliver a high-quality score that meets the client's requirements. This book will show you how to manage a music project efficiently.

Challenges associated with composing soundtracks professionally

If you want to take on jobs composing music for clients, there is a list of challenges that you'll need to deal with. From day one, you're expected to:

- Know how to find composing jobs. Such jobs aren't usually listed like traditional jobs.

- Once you identify a potential gig, you need to know how to market and sell yourself to clients to gain work.

- You need to know how to use a wide array of music production software. Music software has undergone a revolution in the last few decades as music production has become significantly less hardware-focused and much more software-driven. The software landscape is constantly changing as new features and plugins appear monthly.

- You need to understand enough music theory to evaluate songs so that you can go and create similar scores to existing music as needed. You need to understand how to craft music to fit desired styles and moods.

- You need the ability to consistently generate production-ready music. You need to have an understanding of composing, recording, mixing, mastering, and how all of this relates to your client's project.

- If composing for game development, you may need to understand the intricacies of adapting music to video game environments.

Whew! That sounds like a lot of stuff to learn. You may feel a little overwhelmed in the beginning, and that's only natural. This book will help you navigate all these challenges. By the time you're done, you'll have a solid introduction to the tools and techniques to do all the above and much more.

Thinking like a composer

There are many challenges you can expect to face when composing. You can break down all of these challenges into a series of steps. You don't have to do all the steps at the same time. Each step on its own could be a specialist aspect and many people have careers focusing on just a single part.

Although this book goes into minute detail about each stage and technical tools and skills, the goal of a composer isn't to become a master technician. The goal of a composer is to create music that fits the project, whatever that may be. On large-scale projects, most technical tasks might even be delegated to specialized personnel to take care of.

You can hire other people to play instruments and mix and master your music. All of that is important, but the composer's job is a bigger picture than mere technical details. A film director's job is to shape the vision of the film and take steps to bring it to life. Like a director, the composer's job is to shape the vision of the music and take steps to bring it to life.

Depending on the project, you may have different teams, instruments, software, and hardware available to you. All this changes due to the nature of the project, or due to technological advances. The playing field is constantly changing, so you should be prepared to adapt to it. In other words, although you do need to know how to use tools to get the job done, you don't need to be an expert before you start and shouldn't get overly attached to any single tool.

It's easy to get hung up on technical details, but they are just one piece of several in the big picture of composing. What is important is that you understand the key stages and can put the pieces together even if you aren't an expert in a particular aspect.

Your job is to deliver music that satisfies the project's requirements. Communicate with the client throughout to understand what they need. Understand how all the pieces fit together so you can jump in wherever necessary. This book is designed to show you how all the pieces fit together.

What this book covers

This book is organized so you can jump around from chapter to chapter to grab the tools required for your project. It is arranged in a logical sequential order, but most of the topics can be learned independently:

Chapter 1, The Business of Composing for Clients, gives you the street smarts you need to get hired for composing jobs. You'll learn how to land composing gigs, learn about networking and get advice on marketing. You'll learn how to deliver a film or game score in a professional way when working with clients.

Chapter 2, Navigating Through the Key Features of FL Studio, introduces you to the digital audio workstation, **FL Studio**. Here, you'll learn the key tools of FL Studio, including the Channel rack, Piano roll, the Playlist, the Mixer, and the Browser. You'll learn how to record audio in FL Studio and how to export music from the software.

Chapter 3, Designing Music with Themes, Leitmotifs, and Scales, provides you with the music theory to give you a solid foundation for composing songs. Here, you'll learn how to use themes, motifs, and leitmotifs to make your music connect with your movie or game project vision. You'll learn how to use scales, modes, and the circle of fifths chord wheel to give structure to your music arrangements.

Chapter 4, Orchestral MIDI Composing, shows you how to create music for orchestral instruments. You'll learn how to make software plugin instruments sound just like live instruments. You'll learn techniques you can use to compose for string instruments, such as violins, violas, cellos, and basses. You'll learn how to compose MIDI for orchestral chord progressions and considerations for mixing orchestral instruments.

Chapter 5, Creating Sheet Music with MuseScore, Scoring with Fruity Video Player, and Diegetic Music, shows you how to create sheet music from any FL Studio project with ease so live musicians can read and play your music. You'll also learn how to use **Fruity Video Player**. If you want to compose for films or video game cut scenes, Fruity Video Player lets you sync music to visuals. Then you'll learn about designing sound effects.

Chapter 6, Influencing Mood with Music and Designing Emotional Music, explores how to compose music for a variety of genres. You'll learn how to compose music that scares your listener, such as music for horror films and games. You'll learn how to design terrifying jump scares, as well as how to compose happy music, sad music, romantic music, and how to create tension and epic music for trailers.

Chapter 7, Creating Interactive Music for Video Games with Wwise, teaches you how to compose interactive music for video games. You'll learn about the Wwise software and see a demo game with sound integrated into it. You'll learn about the interactive horizontal re-sequencing and vertical remixing music techniques and see how Wwise can be used to implement these techniques. You'll also learn how to create music in FL Studio for use in vertical remixing.

Chapter 8, Soundtrack Composing Templates, provides you with tips for overcoming writer's block. You'll be provided with template lists to make your composing efficient and production-ready. You'll also learn about resources to continue your music journey beyond this book.

How to get the most out of this book

The goal is to create music that fits your visuals while sounding polished. To get the best results, you need to be creating music on a regular basis. Composing music is just like playing an instrument. If you want to get good, you need to practice. Unlike playing an instrument, when you're composing music, you're less focused on the technique and more focused on the end result of how the music fits the project you're composing for.

You need to think in terms of the big picture about how to design a song for specific emotions, how the song fits the visuals, and how everything relates to your client's vision. Do these things well, and you're on your way to becoming a composer.

This book will give you many tips and tricks, but you still need experience to learn. To apply the lessons in this book, you'll benefit most by having a project to compose for. I recommend finding a moving visual that needs music. This could be a video, video game, or live performance. Then you can directly apply and relate the skills you pick up in this book to your own circumstances.

Software/hardware covered in the book	Software website
FL Studio	https://www.image-line.com/
MuseScore	https://musescore.org/en
Wwise	https://www.audiokinetic.com/en/products/wwise

While reading this book, you can share your music and collaborate in the online Facebook group with other readers/students here:

https://www.facebook.com/groups/musicproducerandcomposercommunity

The FL Studio fruit logo is a trademark of Image Line NV and has been used with permission. This is a courtesy and does not constitute any endorsement of this book and its contents by Image Line.

Download the color images

We also provide a PDF file that has color images of the screenshots and diagrams used in this book. You can download it here: https://static.packt-cdn.com/downloads/9781803233291_ColorImages.pdf.

Conventions used

There are a number of text conventions used throughout this book.

Bold: Indicates a new term, an important word, or words that you see on screen. For instance, words in menus or dialog boxes appear in **bold**. Here is an example: "In the preceding screenshot, you'll see a button with **PAT** and **SONG**."

> **Tips or Important Notes**
> Appear like this.

Get in touch

Feedback from our readers is always welcome.

General feedback: If you have questions about any aspect of this book, email us at customercare@packtpub.com and mention the book title in the subject of your message.

Errata: Although we have taken every care to ensure the accuracy of our content, mistakes do happen. If you have found a mistake in this book, we would be grateful if you would report this to us. Please visit www.packtpub.com/support/errata and fill in the form.

Piracy: If you come across any illegal copies of our works in any form on the internet, we would be grateful if you would provide us with the location address or website name. Please contact us at copyright@packt.com with a link to the material.

If you are interested in becoming an author: If there is a topic that you have expertise in and you are interested in either writing or contributing to a book, please visit authors.packtpub.com.

Share Your Thoughts

Once you've read *Music for Film and Game Soundtracks with FL Studio*, we'd love to hear your thoughts! Scan the QR code below to go straight to the Amazon review page for this book and share your feedback.

https://www.amazon.in/review/create-review/error?asin=%3C180323329X%3E

Your review is important to us and the tech community and will help us make sure we're delivering excellent quality content.

Part 1: The Business of Composing for Clients

This section will introduce you to the business side of composing for clients, including how to deal with clients and organize and plan soundtrack projects.

We will cover the following chapter in this section:

- *Chapter 1, The Business of Composing for Clients*

1
The Business of Composing for Clients

In this chapter, you will learn about the business of composing music for clients. We will discuss how to land a job composing music so you can get started, how to prepare for meetings with clients, and how to obtain actionable project requirements. This way, you'll be able to strategically satisfy your clients every time.

We will discuss planning a film score and useful methods for collaborating with other musicians so that you can work efficiently. Finally, we will discuss how to collect music royalty revenue so you can earn passive income from your compositions.

We will cover the following topics in this chapter:

- Landing your first composing gig
- Preparing for meeting clients
- Planning a music score
- Collaborating with others
- Advice for avoiding rookie mistakes
- The day-to-day tasks of composing

Landing your first composing gig

Landing a job creating music for clients is not like getting a regular office job. Music jobs are rarely posted on job boards and the interview is different from traditional interviews. This is for a good reason. The task of composing music requires a very specific set of traits that are not easily evaluated by reading a resume or asking traditional interview questions.

Let's take a moment to put ourselves in the client's shoes. Imagine you're a director who has just finished creating a movie. You've spent time carefully revising a script, running casting calls to find actors who look the part and have the right chemistry, scouting filming locations, and planning shoots, and are finally in the process of editing the footage in postproduction. You now need scenes in your film to hit certain emotions, and you need music that's tailored just right to do this.

After expending all that effort trying to make sure every detail fits the film precisely, do you think you would hire someone you've never met to make the music? Perhaps if they're famous with a solid track record you might. But if you haven't heard of them before, then you're going to need some evidence to prove they can deliver. You need to trust that whatever music is composed will be aligned with the overall style of the film. That information can't be obtained by reading a resume or asking traditional interview questions.

When a client needs someone to compose music for their project, the first thing they do is think about their current connections. Is there someone they already know who can do the job? With the exception of music videos, the music doesn't come first—the project comes first…which means the music is often an afterthought. An important afterthought, but if there is no project, then no one is asking for music.

What does this mean? It means that the best odds of you landing a music job is being already known by the people creating projects. Ideally, they should know about you long before they start looking for someone to compose music. If you want to compose music for films, you should be hanging around with people who are actively making films. If you want to compose music for video games, you need to be hanging out with people who are making video games.

Figure out which films or video games are getting created locally and find ways to enter those communities. Learn everything you can about the projects getting created. Ask questions, explore their past projects, and volunteer to help with their projects in any way that you can. The more you can do to establish your presence, the more natural it will be for you to compose music for them. Of course, you also need to establish yourself as a capable and professional music composer.

How to establish yourself as a professional

What should you do before you start applying for composing jobs? You should do everything you can to establish a brand portraying you as a capable music-composing professional. There are lots of musicians out there—only a subset of them can make original music for other people in a professional setting. You want potential clients to know that you are part of that special group.

Many good live musicians don't have the skills to be good composers, while many composers aren't great live musicians. There's overlap for sure, but there is also a separate composer skillset that is required to do composing that is much more than being good at playing music. Not to worry, though—this book will teach you everything you need to know to get your skills up to par.

Here are a few quick steps to make you appear instantly more professional to potential clients:

- Have a professional-looking music website that displays your music and music-creating services. The website should at a minimum have samples of your music, a short biography about you, and your contact information.

- Have your past music easily accessible so you can provide it at a moment's notice. I personally use SoundCloud as my site of choice when I need to provide links to my portfolio. SoundCloud is a website where you can upload your music, and listeners can listen to it without having to log in.

  To learn more about SoundCloud, visit `https://soundcloud.com`.

- Get business cards. Even though people don't need business cards anymore when contact information can be plugged into your phone, a business card makes people think you're serious about what you do. Business cards are also convenient to hand out at events. If you don't have business cards already, go make some.

- Create an email account dedicated to music business-related activities. Make sure your email address sounds professional.

- Create a Facebook page dedicated to your music-related business. When you share a post saying that you made music for a project, it acts as free advertisement for you.

- Even better than a Facebook page, create a local community group or Facebook group related to your music business. When I was in university, I wanted to create films, but there weren't any film-making groups on campus. So, I created my own. This helped to foster a community of filmmakers and gave me opportunities to get started creating my music portfolio. I was also lucky enough to enroll in classes about creating video games, which gave me my first shot at composing for games. If you're a student, you have a golden opportunity to organize student groups around music/films/video games. There are always lots of like-minded people eager to join as members. Make the most of these student opportunities while you can.

Next, let's talk about networking.

How to network

If you want to compose, you should be going to meetup events where films and games are being planned. Find out where the producers, filmmakers, actors, and writers are gathering.

If you're interested in finding existing groups or creating a local community group, consider checking out the following website: `https://meetup.com/`. Meetup is a website that helps you find or host local events. Sometimes, you can find film- or video game-related events near you. If they aren't any nearby, consider starting a Meetup group yourself.

Another good place to start networking is at amateur film festivals, where there are always parties for meeting and greeting. Meet and greets at festivals may not be specifically listed on the event brochure. If so, ask around at the event, and you'll invariably discover that some members are going for refreshments afterward. At meet and greets, give your business card to everyone before you leave, and get their contact information. Do everything you can to make friends with the people who are the project creators.

After the event, send a text or email reminding people of who you are, something relevant to the conversation you had with them, and that you'd like to follow up. Perhaps send them a link to a song you made. Then, routinely follow up with them on a regular basis by calling or sending them a message to keep up to date with their activities. I have always found the atmosphere at amateur film festivals to be inclusive and welcoming to newcomers, so if you're new, this is a good place to start.

It's unlikely that meeting someone at a meet-and-greet event will land you a job outright. I've never seen that happen at a first meeting. It's always a series of bumping into the same people at several events until people eventually begin to recognize your face. Each time they see you, it becomes easier to make yourself relevant to their project. Then, when you feel it's time, mention you have some music you'd like to send to them for consideration.

Don't know what to do at these events to get started when networking or how to break the ice? Here are some safe conversation starters:

* I find it's often good to play the *new-in-town* card. People like to introduce new people to events. You can ask what the host likes about the event and how they got into it and ask who's attending and whether you can be introduced to them. Even if you've been to a particular event once or twice before, sometimes it still helps to pretend that you'd like to be introduced around as this can make it easier to enter into a new circle.

* *What project are you working on at the moment?* Be genuinely curious and find out any details that you can about their project. People like to brag. When they brag, you can learn a lot if you listen.

- *How did you get into ____?* For example, directing, producing, writing, game making, and so on.

You can volunteer to help organize existing networking events; this is an easy way to get your foot in the door and make yourself relevant. It might even give you the opportunity to show off some of your past work. Perhaps you can find some excuse for a demonstration to show off your past projects. If there's some way you can make a short presentation, it's a guaranteed way to get your face recognized at an event.

What if I don't already have a portfolio of music?

In order to get a composing gig, you usually need to have some previous music-composing experience. People want to see what you've created in the past before they can trust you. In the beginning, it may feel like a nasty loop you're stuck in. You need work to get experience, but you need experience to get work. What if you don't have any past work to point at? Then, you may need to create some work for yourself. Sign up to create films for amateur film festivals. Go to these film festivals and try to recruit people who are interested in creating a short film. These people may turn out to be looking to hire a composer further down the road or—more likely—happen to know an event to attend or someone who happens to be working on a project.

There are lots of film contests that are open to the public. If you're interested in submitting films to film festivals, the following website lists festivals, contact information, and submission criteria to enter into them: `https://filmfreeway.com/`. You can see a screenshot from the FilmFreeway website here:

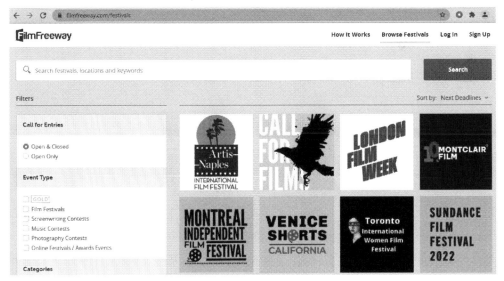

Figure 1.1 – FilmFreeway

The FilmFreeway website has filters that help you narrow down the type of film that you want to participate in. You can filter for entry fees, countries, dates, and submission deadlines. The website breaks down film festivals into the following categories to make it easy to find the type of film you're interested in:

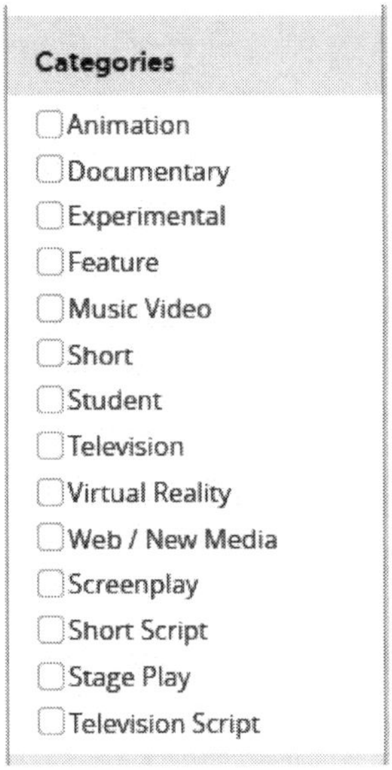

Categories

- Animation
- Documentary
- Experimental
- Feature
- Music Video
- Short
- Student
- Television
- Virtual Reality
- Web / New Media
- Screenplay
- Short Script
- Stage Play
- Television Script

Figure 1.2 – FilmFreeway Categories

In addition to **Categories**, you can also filter by the film's genre/focus:

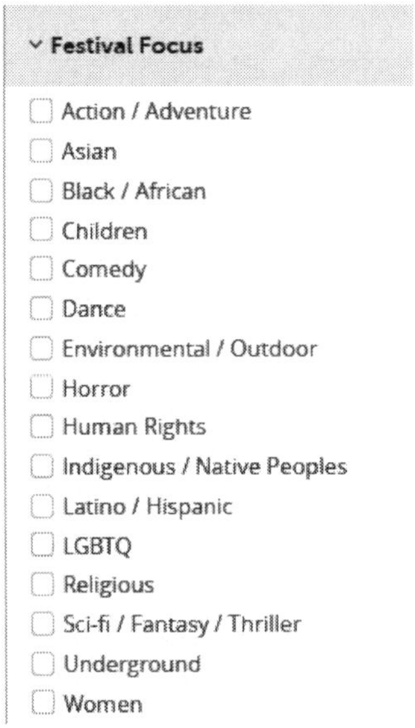

Festival Focus

- Action / Adventure
- Asian
- Black / African
- Children
- Comedy
- Dance
- Environmental / Outdoor
- Horror
- Human Rights
- Indigenous / Native Peoples
- Latino / Hispanic
- LGBTQ
- Religious
- Sci-fi / Fantasy / Thriller
- Underground
- Women

Figure 1.3 – FilmFreeway Festival Focus

If you're looking to find film festivals to participate in, FilmFreeway is an excellent resource.

In recent years, I've found Facebook to be a useful tool for cold calling. On Facebook, you can join Facebook groups dedicated to your local film- and game-making community. In these groups, you can see postings from people networking and making film role-call postings. I've found that messaging people in these groups can sometimes lead to gigs or referrals. Even if a post is only to recruit actors, applying with an email describing the services you offer can sometimes get your foot in the door. On several occasions, I've found that applying as a composer to an actor role call has led to an opportunity.

When you find a contact who is in need of music, you need to find a way to show that you are the best person for the job. If you send a generic resume, you're probably not going to get the job. Before applying, research everything about the project you can find. When sending an initial message to the client, explain how you can create music that is tailored to their project. Then, go and create some demo music that you think would fit their project. Best-case scenario—the creator loves the demo music, and you have a starting musical idea to build off of. Worst-case scenario—you created some music for free that you can add to your portfolio. But if you're reading this book, it means you love making music, so you should think of this as fun rather than being a burden. The goal is to get a job making music. How do you get that job? You make music. See, you're already winning!

A worthy mention is the following website: `https://soundbetter.com/`. You can see a screenshot from the SoundBetter website here:

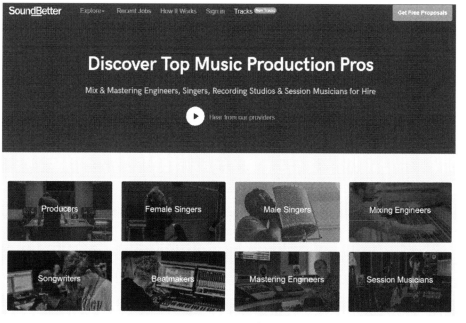

Figure 1.4 – SoundBetter

The SoundBetter website allows you to hire or sell music-related services. You can list your services for hire on this site. There's a section of the site dedicated to music job postings.

Landing a composing gig is hard if you approach it through traditional job search methods. Composing gigs are rarely advertised to the public. If you're looking for job postings to send your resume, you're probably going to have a hard time. Most composing gigs come from established networks. They come from people who already know you and your work. You need to go and establish relationships with people who are actively creating music-related projects long before they need music.

The good news is that once you've landed one gig, the client will often use your services time and time again, and it'll be much easier to find referrals for further projects.

Preparing for meeting clients

What you'll soon discover going into interviews with clients is they often don't know what they're looking for in a soundtrack. Sometimes, the client thinks they know what they want, but they aren't musicians themselves and often have no idea how to make music. They might know what they like and have a vision of what it might sound like, but that's like pointing at a piece of art and saying, *I want something just like that...but also tailored toward my preferences.* Very vague. You're getting hired by someone who doesn't know how to do the job themselves...and they're super picky about the work delivered.

Landing a composing job with a client requires the ability to translate the client's vision into musical ideas and explain it to the client without using music terminology. To get hired, you need to demonstrate you have the skills to do this when you're pitching yourself for a client's project. It's your job to figure out what the client wants and to guide them along the way if they aren't sure. If the client claims they know what kind of music they want, it's your job to get it out of them and articulate it to all parties.

The person who can best figure out what the client wants and explain it clearly back to them is a likely candidate to get the job. This is also the reason that directors usually rely on composers they've worked with before—they know they can trust their composer to deliver an idea that meets their vision. So, the conversation with the client is a lot about building trust and rapport. In order to get them to trust you, you have to show them that you're genuinely curious and interested in their project.

Don't play hard to get at this stage. It's too early on to think about money. In fact, I recommend not bringing up the topic of money until the client has already decided that they want you for the project. You want to get as many details as you can, show that you're capable, and have a plan of attack as to how you'll add value to the film. If you simply list off a price before the client sees the value you bring, then you might put yourself into a bidding war for the lowest price with other composers.

The price you can charge a client depends on the following factors:

- The client's budget.

- The size of the project (for example, number of songs/length required).

- Your track record. If you have a strong portfolio or reputation, it's easier to charge more.

- Expenses that are required to create a score (for example, hiring musicians, recording sessions, and equipment rentals).

- The value your music adds to the project.

You might ask, *How much is this value?* Well, art is subjective, and the value that music adds to any project is assessed differently every time It's up to you to convince the client your music has value. Lots of value. Yes—you might put a number of hours into a project and arbitrarily assign an hourly rate, but how much to price those work hours is up to negotiation. Whatever amount you can convince the client of, you can charge.

A lot of composing gigs are freelance contracts. As a general rule of thumb, as a freelance contractor, it's smarter to charge a high price per hour. For example, let's say the client has a budget of $500 (US dollars). You might say, *I'll charge $50/hour for 10 hours to get the job done*, rather than saying you need *$10/hour for 50 hours*. You get $500 either way, but in the first approach, if something happens and the client needs more music, the client will respect your time a lot more than they will in the second scenario. In order to charge a higher price, you need to come across as a professional. The more capable and professional you come across, the more reasonable your price will seem to the client.

We've discussed landing a job with a client. Next, let's discuss what to do once you've got the gig.

Planning a music score

Getting the planning right for a music score is a crucial part of the job. The more prepared and detailed your plan, the easier it will be to do the job. Careful planning acts as a safeguard checklist to ensure you correctly gathered all the requirements needed and didn't forget anything. The first part of planning a music score is gathering client requirements in a document that we'll refer to as the **music design document**.

During your interviews with clients, you'll want to write down as much detail as you can in this document. There are a number of key items you will want to consider putting in the document. What follows are some suggestions.

Composing for films

For film music, you'll break down each scene into significant events to determine what kinds of sounds are required. Here are some items you'll want to account for:

- What emotion/tone/mood does the director want?

- What's the intensity of the scene?

- Is there dialogue in the scene?

- What Foley sounds are present (sounds that are part of the actual scene)?

List out the ideas you have and what you have in mind for the client. If you need specific instruments, equipment, session musicians, and so on, you can list your requirements here. You can use the music design document as a sort of proposal to get approval if you need to ask for a music budget later.

Composing for video games

For video games, the composer is usually brought into the development phase much earlier than in films. You will likely only have concept art to work on to get an idea of what the game could look like. The music can help to set the emotional tone and may influence other design aspects of the game, so your music may have a large influence on the design of the game itself. Many games incorporate music as part of the gameplay.

Video games have a variety of events that require music, and these requirements need to be gathered and itemized in the planning stage. Examples of situations requiring music in games include the following:

- Menus

- Loading level screens

- Entering new levels

- Completing levels

- Music for each boss

- Entering new rooms

- Obtaining items

- Unlocking achievements

- Ambient sounds for environments
- Battle sounds
- Cutscenes
- Music that characters are listening to within the game
- Winning the game
- Losing the game

The nature of your involvement may vary depending on the type of game. Most video games have a variety of cutscenes that require music. You can treat these cutscenes as you would any film score.

For some video games, you may be involved in more of the development of the game. You may have to design interactive music that changes throughout the game. If composing interactive music, you'll need a much more comprehensive music design document. The document will need to keep track of how music changes throughout the levels. If there are layers of music that are played on top of each other, the design document could specify conditions where these music layers are added. You will want to keep this document maintained and up to date each time you complete a piece of music for the project.

We discuss music for video games in more detail in *Chapter 7, Creating Interactive Music for Video Games with Wwise.*

Gathering soundtrack requirements for the design document

For film projects, composers are usually brought in after filming has commenced or been completed and is in the postproduction stage. This usually means there is a rough cut of gathering for the design document. It may be missing audio, but there are some visuals for you to get an idea of what the film will look like. This makes everything significantly easier because you can see how pieces fit together, how long each song should be, and the key moments the music needs to hit.

If the client provided you with a rough cut of the video, they'll usually give you suggested timings for when music could be played. For video games, there will usually be an itemized list you or the client will create for each thing/level/environment requiring sound.

Temp music is music that has been temporarily placed in a film or game to give the viewer an idea of what the music could sound like. It's usually music that was composed for other films or video games that the client likes. Composers have a conflicting view of temp music. On one hand, it gives an idea of what the director has in mind. On the other hand, it could cause you or the director to get so attached to the temp music that you try to compose music mimicking it. This is a trap that's easy to fall into. Trying to recreate a great piece of music used in another film is not a task you want to be doing. If the temp music is perfect, then they don't need you to compose anything else. You may as well just use the temp music. You want to be inspired by the temp music, and then go out and create something original.

Consider how the temp music adds value to the film and where it's lacking. Don't accept the temp music as a requirement for the project at face value—it's just a placeholder. You should ask the director why they chose each temp track and figure out what their intention was for the chosen piece. It could be that the director wants a certain emotion or intensity, but you won't know for sure unless you ask.

There's a quote sometimes attributed to Pablo Picasso: *Good artists borrow, great artists steal.* Let's discuss how to "steal" ideas in the right way. Listening to temp music and copying is, of course, bad practice. However, if you take ideas from multiple songs and combine them in a new way, you're no longer stealing—now, you're being inspired. Take the idea that you want to copy, then find a few more ideas that you want to copy, and finally, create a hybrid of the bunch.

Watching the film with the client

Arrange a time to sit down with the client and watch the film together, stopping at moments where music should come in. Discuss the emotional tone that should be delivered by the music at key moments in the film. When I do this, as we're watching, I'll have my laptop out and will furiously type down notes, timings for the film, desired emotions, and any comments that come up in conversation.

Most of the time, in client conversations, you'll explain music using examples as a reference—references such as other famous movies and descriptions of iconic scenes. You'll probably never discuss music theory with the client. More likely, you'll discuss how a scene makes the client feel. What is it about the scene that makes them feel that way?

If the director provided temp music, I'll go through and write the timings for each temp music track. Any notes and thoughts that come to mind while watching the footage I'll record down.

After the meeting, I'll collect the notes, organize the thoughts in a logical manner, and rewrite them into the design document.

Once the design document is done and approved, it's then time to create a document I like to call the **Soundtrack Planner**. This document will schedule the entire music score for the project. It will take all the requirements that we identified in the design document and itemize everything into actionable pieces. The Soundtrack Planner document will also serve to be the communication tool to help all parties plan the music score.

Creating a Soundtrack Planner

How do you organize a film score? If it were a single song, you might not need much planning. But we're not talking about a single song. We're talking about dozens, potentially hundreds of different pieces of sound. If you're working on a video game soundtrack, you might need to keep track of programming consideration details as well.

When you get feedback from the client for your music, it's not as simple as just asking an opinion. You'll get an answer, but it might not be something you know how to act upon. You need to have a logical method to keep track of all suggestions and changes and formulate them into actionable steps you can carry out.

If you're looking at a big-budget film, the company may have some sort of ticket-tracking software they want to use. More often, though, the client leaves you in charge of organizing your own score.

I personally find that a good old Google Drive document or SharePoint shared document is simple and does the job. Most people already know how to use shared drive documents, so you don't have to worry about the client not knowing how to use the software.

You can share a link to the editable document with the director and crew. Everyone has access to the same document, so everyone can always see the latest version. Make sure you keep a backup copy of the document at regular intervals just in case someone comes in and accidentally messes everything up.

Here's an example of a Soundtrack Planner that I used for a client. I included a **Time** column showing the suggested location to place the music in the film, a column with the filename of the song, a column for a description of the song requirements, a column for the song status, and columns for comments from the client and composer:

Time	File Name	Director's Notes	Song Status	Director's Feedback/Suggestions	Composer Comments
04:30	04:30 - Fall	Tone should be sad, remorseful, dark	Approved	Done. Beautiful	Sounds like you already have all you need. Let me know if you need anything else for this piece.
08.20	08.20 - Nostalgia long version	Tone should be unobtrusive. Blend into the background. Slight droning.	Awaiting Approval	The version without the rubber-band sound seems to have a slight click every time the chord changes. Other than that, it's great. Can we add whatever that subtle drone sound is that kicks in in the "Goodbye song" around the 48sec mark? The "Nostalgia" song with the rubber sound is perfect. And we'll make adjustment during sound mix	Added Another version: "08.20 - Nostalgia V2" with your requested changes
20:32-20:56	20:32- Drone	-Atonal -Anticipation - Atmosphere -Droning	Needs revisions	Ambient, natural tone. Needs to give the emotion of uncertainty	
46.00-48.24	46.00 - Boss Fight	48.17 excitement dies down	In Progress		

Figure 1.5 – Soundtrack planner

In the document, I include a legend that's color-coded to make it easy for the director to understand the status each song is currently in. For example, I use white for **In Progress**, yellow for **Awaiting Approval**, green for **Approved/Done**, and red for **Needs Revisions**, as illustrated here:

Yellow:	Green:	Red:	White
Awaiting Approval	Approved/Done	Needs Revisions	In Progress

Figure 1.6 – Soundtrack planner legend

If the director were to quickly glance at this table, they would be able to get an idea of the status for each song in the project. Whenever I make progress on the songs, I'll update the shared drive with the songs and update the document with the relevant information. Then, I'll send a link with the shared document to the director to let them know some changes were made.

If you don't use an organized method for your score, it's very easy to lose track of what work has already been done. Make sure you name your filenames in an easy-to-understand method. I like to include the song name and a suggested timing for the song in the film. For example, I might call a song `00.46.00 - Boss Fight - Version 3`.

This title lets the director know where to place the music timewise in the film, what the scene is about, and the current song version so that they can make sure they're using the latest version. You might also want to consider including the song tempo and song key in the name.

You want to make it as little work as possible for the director to use your music. If the director is losing track of where your music is, unsure which song goes where in the film, what the status of a song's progress is, or which version of a song they should be using, this means your music could be organized more effectively.

If you do your job right, the director should be able to open the Soundtrack Planner and instantly know what work has been done. They can then open a folder containing your music and easily navigate through the folder structure to find your song. The song should be labeled in such a way that the director knows exactly what it is and how to use it based on the comments in the Soundtrack Planner.

I've received positive feedback from directors in the past saying they really liked this Soundtrack Planner method of organizing music. They said they found it clear and easy to use and that it helped them know how the project is coming along and how much more work needs to be done.

Researching music ideas for the project

Once you've got the outline for your Soundtrack Planner, the fun part now begins: the research for musical ideas. You have your soundtrack requirements; now, you need to go out into the field and get inspired. It's time to create an inspiration board of resources to draw from.

I usually look up music in movies or games that were discussed with the client during conversations. I'll review the temp music used. I'll pay special attention to the instruments. I'll note the style and see whether I can dig up information on which tools and software techniques were used. The goal isn't to recreate the sounds but to get ideas about what has been done before so you have the information to hand if you need it later.

Clips from films and games can always be found online on YouTube. I'll create a document filled with links and descriptions of relevant clips. If I need inspiration for a scene, I can use this document for reference.

If I have time, I may spend effort curating original sounds and instruments. Some composers go around recording sounds on their phones. They can then use the sounds as audio samples and manipulate the samples into whatever they need.

I personally like to search for new genres of music that I normally wouldn't listen to—sounds that pull me out of my comfort zone often give me ideas for composing. When I'm not composing, I'm usually listening to electronic dance music. But when I'm composing for clients, I'll go on adventures seeking out unusual blends of sounds I'd normally never listen to. The weirder, the better. If it's a style of music I've never heard before, that really piques my attention.

At some point, you're going to run into writer's block. At these times, it's imperative you have something to turn to so that you can get your ideas flowing again. Having done your research beforehand and having a reference document on hand will help get the creative juices flowing when you need it. We'll cover many more tips for coming up with ideas for music composing in *Chapter 3*, *Designing Music with Themes, Leitmotifs, and Scales*, and we'll learn how to overcome writer's block in *Chapter 8*, *Soundtrack Composing Templates*.

In this section, we learned how to plan a film score. We also learned a method for researching your project. We learned how to organize your score using a Soundtrack Planner to help you and your client keep track of your music.

Next, let's learn how to collaborate on group projects with additional composers. This next tip is slightly more advanced and will likely be more relevant when you work on larger projects rather than when you're first starting out.

Collaborating with others

Sharing your music with collaborators requires organization and planning. If you're prepared, sharing your projects and music can be a relatively easy experience.

Make sure your music is in a format easily understood by your team members. You'll have to come up with an agreed-upon folder structure of files and formats. Talk about this beforehand to make sure that everyone understands how to locate the music.

Make it easy for collaborators to know what your music is just by reading the file- and folder-naming structure. Consider labeling folders with information such as the following:

- Filenames and formats
- The genre of the music
- The tempo and song key
- Instrumentation

Problems with collaborating

When collaborating with other composers, you'll soon encounter the difficulties of trying to share project files and keeping track of the latest file. If someone else needs to access your music project file and they don't have access to your computer, what can they do?

First, think about what happens if you send the entire project file to someone else. If they try to open up the project and don't have the same digital audio workstation as you, they won't be able to open it directly as their project files will be incompatible.

If they do have the same digital audio workstation as you but don't have the same instrument plugins installed, they'll be able to open the project but still won't be able to use it because plugins will be missing. This will result in an annoying error screen, such as the following:

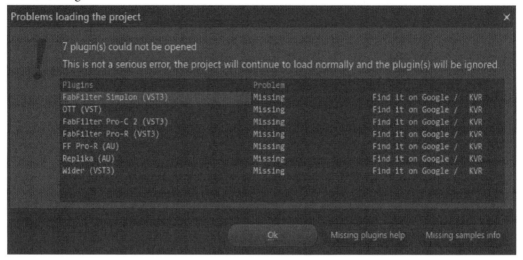

Figure 1.7 – Opening projects with missing plugins

Trying to navigate missing plugins is a nightmare. You have to figure out what plugins are missing. Then you have to try to recreate the settings used. Not fun!

These problems come up all the time if you don't communicate in advance. This is easy to overlook if you haven't collaborated with another musician before, but it can cause you many hours of frustration and is easy to avoid. To avoid all of this, make sure you figure out and agree upon which digital audio workstation and plugins you and your collaborators will have access to before you begin. Make sure you only use plugins that all parties have access to.

Version control with Splice

What if you and your collaborators are using different digital audio workstations? This means you won't be able to send the entire project file, since the collaborators won't be able to open it. If that's the case, you're going to need to plan to export audio stems from your project each time you want to send music to someone else.

If you are both using the same digital audio workstation, then collaborating is much easier. But you'll still need to figure out which instrument and effect plugins you both have access to. Then, you'll need to have a discussion about how to update each other on changes when you make them—for example, send each other a message each time you make changes to your music project to let the other know there's a new project version.

Have I lost you yet? If this sounds confusing, it's because it is. Trying to figure out the latest version of a project file is tedious and messy. Fortunately, there is a solution: version control software. Software developers figured out that there needed to be a way to manage file versions long before musicians did. Using version control software such as Git is now mandatory for most programmers.

In recent years, version control software has emerged for musicians too. One of the most popular music version control software solutions is called **Splice**. It allows you to save your project at different stages in a remote repository and open up previous versions of your project. Most importantly, you can share your Splice project file with collaborators so that they have access to the latest project version at all times.

> **Note**
> You can download Splice for free at `https://splice.com`.

Once in Splice, you can share the project file with your collaborators' Splice accounts, and they'll gain access to all the versions of the project file. The following screenshot shows the Splice home page:

Figure 1.8 – Splice site

At the time of writing, Splice doesn't have the ability to merge changes between file versions like Git does, so only one of you will be able to make changes at a time to the newest project version. You won't be able to make changes simultaneously. This means that each time you plan to work on the project file, it's essential that you log in to Splice and open up the most recent version of the project. If you don't do this, you'll probably find yourself working on an outdated version of the project file.

Splice also offers a library of royalty-free sounds that you can pay for and use in your projects. It also allows you to rent instrument plugins until you've paid off the amount that it would take to originally buy the plugin and lets you own it afterward. So, if you're strapped for cash at the moment but need plugin equipment, this may be a handy alternative to buying instrument plugins outright.

When you log in to Splice, you'll see a screen similar to this:

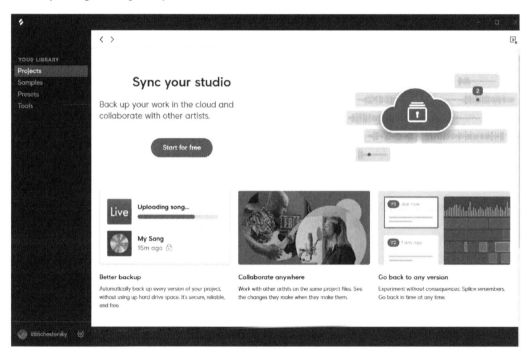

Figure 1.9 – Splice dashboard

On the left-side panel, you'll see the ability to navigate to your project, download samples, or see tools available in Splice.

Each time you save your project, Splice will add a new version to the repository. You can add comments to individual tracks for collaborators to see. If you are using the same digital audio workstation, you can open up the project file from Splice and it will automatically keep your project files in sync going forward. The following screenshot shows an example of Splice Studio, which allows you to manage song versions:

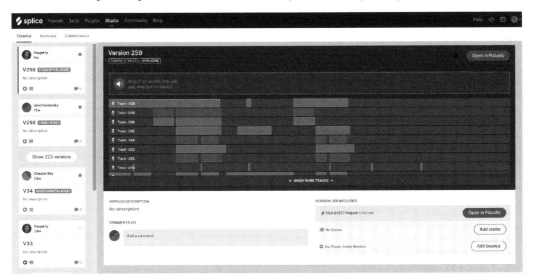

Figure 1.10 – Splice versions

In the preceding screenshot, you can see an example of how Splice displays your project for collaboration. On the left side, it lists previous versions of the project that you can choose to open. The top middle shows any changes made, and the bottom lets you enter any notes and comments you wish to record.

Using Splice to collaborate with team members can work great if you have solid communication. If you don't have good communication, then you're going to run into problems. Problems come when you start working on a song version that isn't the latest.

Each time you work on a new song version, you need to notify your team members that you are saving a new version. This way, they can remember to open up the new version before making modifications. As long as you're all taking turns working on the latest version, you'll be able to avoid problems.

We've discussed how to share music with collaborators. Next, let's learn some tips for newbies.

Advice for avoiding rookie mistakes

What follows are a few items you might overlook if you're new to composing music.

Get the project in writing

You should have some sort of documentation stating the services you plan on providing for the client before you begin work. This sounds obvious, but when you're starting out, the client may not have a contract drafted up ready for you. If you don't have any documentation to say you have the job, you should assume you don't officially have the job.

The client could easily swap you out with another composer at any moment's notice, and there wouldn't be much you could do about it. If the client doesn't have a contract for you, it's not a problem. Just draft up an invoice and send it to them confirming the fees for your project to seal the deal. Agreeing to something in writing psychologically makes people feel like they're serious about the agreement. It also allows all parties to know what the expectations are of each other to help avoid confusion.

If you're drafting up an invoice, include the following details:

- Contact information of you/your company

- Contact information of the client

- Services you're providing for the client

- Dates for services and/or deadlines

- Itemized pricing for the services or hourly rate, depending on how you want to bill the client

By the time you're drafting up the invoice, you've probably discussed the budget for the project already. The invoice is usually just confirming whatever you already agreed to earlier on. However, if you haven't officially agreed on a price yet, an invoice is a way to make the first offer while at the same time providing reasons to back up why you are charging your prices. You could, for example, list out songs that need creating and assign an expected number of budgeted hours for each.

The nice thing about drafting up your own invoice is you can put on it whatever you want. It's then up to the other party to disagree and request adjustments, but oddly enough, clients rarely do. Usually, whatever you put into an invoice ends up staying.

I've even used invoices to intentionally get myself out of composing gigs I didn't want. One time, a client came to me with an uninteresting assignment that would have been a huge commitment that I didn't have time to do at that moment. Saying no to someone offering a music job is something I always want to avoid. It might burn a bridge with them, and who knows who they are connected with. Instead of saying no, I simply listed out the services as usual on my invoice and itemized each with a very high price that was still justifiable, but unlikely that the client would be willing to pay. It was a way for me to back out of the deal while saving face.

Ask for feedback

One of the biggest mistakes you can run into when composing is not getting enough feedback. Now, this may sound like common sense, but it's not. The way you obtain feedback and adapt is a delicate balancing act. This is a fragile part of the job. If you do it wrong, you'll annoy the people you ask and look like you don't know what you're doing, and no matter how good your music is, you'll create a bad impression. Do it right, and you'll establish trust with the client and be brought back again and again to do more jobs.

Most of the time when playing music, your audience isn't scrutinizing every detail of your song and telling you what they think. Even if you get feedback when playing for a live audience, they probably don't have a specific critique that is easily actionable.

This is not the case when composing for clients. Working with a client is a completely different environment where feedback is everything. If your client says nothing when you hand them music, that doesn't mean they love the music. It means that the client isn't thinking about the music. That's a big distinction.

I made this mistake on my first composing gig. On my very first movie, I composed a soundtrack for the whole film. It took a few months of work. The client said nothing when I sent him the music throughout, and I thought that meant he must like the music. Why would someone hire you for a job and say nothing when you send them the work? It turned out it was because his attention was focused on other things. When I told the client I was done, he said he hadn't listened to any of the music yet. When he put the music in the film, he said he didn't like what he heard. He wanted me to redo the whole thing.

He thought that it was my fault. With some time and distance from the event, when I look back on it, he's right. It's the composer's job to put in the effort to make sure their music is received. Don't let my mistake happen to you. As often as you can, check in with the client and ask for feedback constantly. If they haven't said anything about your music for a while, always assume that they haven't reviewed the music yet and that you need to follow up.

It was because of this experience that I was forced to look into a better approach for planning out my soundtrack scores. After experimenting, I settled upon the Soundtrack Planner method discussed earlier in this chapter. If you keep updating the Soundtrack Planner and notifying the client about your changes, you should be able to collect feedback effectively and guarantee effective communication.

We've discussed advice for rookies. Next, let's discuss what an average day might look like on the job.

The day-to-day tasks of composing

Here's what a typical day might look like when composing. First, I'll check my Soundtrack Planner to see what items need to be completed and what priority they have. I'll also check my design document to see any notes regarding the music.

If I don't already have an idea of what music to make, I'll spend some time reviewing my previous research reference documents. I might have some instruments I want to use, references that inspire me, or a visual to get me in the right frame of mind.

If it's a film or game cutscene, I'll set markers for the video footage in my digital audio workstation. I'll put labels onto key moments to visually keep track of events the music needs to hit. We'll cover this in detail in *Chapter 5, Creating Sheet Music with MuseScore, Scoring with Fruity Video Player, and Diegetic Music.* I like to have a separate project file for each scene, although I will duplicate project files and reuse the instruments and effects loaded.

Next, I need a sound I think will work for the scene. This is where the fun and experimentation begin. I'm a piano guy, so I usually start with finding chords. I'll try to figure out a chord progression that gives me the tone I want for the scene. This takes me a while, and I'll go through several iterations because I feel strongly that chord progressions are the foundation of whether a song sounds good in the end or not. Some composers aren't as picky about the chords early on and prefer to identify a specific sound that fits the scene. There are many ways to start and there are many right answers. We'll cover lots of suggestions for coming up with musical ideas in *Chapter 3, Designing Music with Themes, Leitmotifs, and Scales.*

Once I'm happy with my chord progression, I'll begin identifying instrumentation for the song. I'll assign melodies in my chord progression to different instruments. I'll layer on instruments. I'll play around with breaking up chords to add some rhythm. I'll tweak the arrangement to hit the various timing marks. By the end, ideally, I'll have several variations of each song.

Composing and arranging the song is the first part. Afterward you need to think about mixing and mastering the song. Sometimes, I want to send an unmixed piece to the client first to get feedback before pouring more hours into something they potentially may not like.

For mixing, I'll segment the instruments into different mix busses based on the frequency range. I'll then apply equalization and compression to isolate/enhance the instruments. I'll try to make instrument frequencies not compete with each other. I may add effects, such as reverb. I'll balance out the volume levels for the instruments.

If you want to learn the ins and outs of mixing with FL Studio, check out my book *The Music Producer's Ultimate Guide to FL Studio 20*:

```
https://www.amazon.ca/Music-Producers-Ultimate-Guide-Studio/
dp/1800565321
```

Once I have some song drafts I'm happy with, I'll export the song and label and organize it so that the client can easily identify what it should be used for. I'll upload it to a shared drive folder. I'll make some notes in the Soundtrack Planner to update it with information about any new songs. Then, I may send a little message to the client, letting them know there's some new music to be reviewed.

At regular intervals, there will also be meetings or phone/video calls with the client to discuss the client's vision for the project and review music to collect feedback. With any feedback, I'll take notes in the music design document to use for reference moving forward.

We've learned about the daily tasks of composing; next, let's learn how to collect revenue from music royalties.

How to collect music royalties

Some client projects pay you through a fixed rate whereby you sign over all the rights for your music. When you're working on a low-budget independent film, you have significantly more negotiating power than when working with large studios. Sometimes (especially if they're hiring you for cheap), you can negotiate so that the client only gets the rights to use your music but you get to keep the ownership rights. This means you can reuse and profit off the music outside of the client's project.

If you can keep ownership rights, you can register your music to collect music royalties. That way, the music you create will generate additional revenue for you whenever someone plays it.

How revenue gets collected for music plays can be very complex. Different regions around the world have different organizations that collect revenue. Trying to keep track of when a song of yours was played on a radio station would be impossible to do yourself. Thankfully, you don't have to.

There are several organizations tasked with collecting revenue from music plays and allocating the music revenue back to creators. These organizations do take a small cut of the revenue, but you wouldn't be able to collect the money without them, so you don't really have a choice.

One kind of royalty to be collected is called **reproduction royalties**, also known as **mechanical royalties**. Whenever your song is placed in a digital file, such as for online music distribution, this is a reproduction, and you are owed royalties for the play.

To collect reproduction royalties in the **United States (US)**, you would use a performing-rights organization, such as the **American Society of Composers, Authors and Publishers (ASCAP)**, **Broadcast Music, Inc. (BMI)**, or the **Society of European Stage Authors and Composers (SESAC)**. You can only join SESAC by invitation, though.

You'll pick one of these organizations and register each of your songs with them. The organization will then collect royalty revenue for you. If you're in a different country, you'll want to check the designated collection body for that region.

Information about ASCAP is available at `https://www.ascap.com/`. You can see their logo here:

Figure 1.11 – ASCAP

Information about BMI is available at `https://www.bmi.com/`. Their logo is shown here:

Figure 1.12 – BMI

There are also public performance royalties. Whenever a song is played on the radio, on television, in a theatre, or at a concert, this is a performance royalty. If you are in the US and you're a performing artist and/or own the master recordings, you'll use an organization called **SoundExchange** to collect royalties. This organization collects and distributes performance royalties to the owners of the rights. If you're in another country, there may be a different organization that you'll need to register with.

Information about SoundExchange is available at `https://www.soundexchange.com/`. Their logo is shown here:

Figure 1.13 – SoundExchange

What about online stores? There are lots of online stores and streaming platforms that can sell your music. Here's a list of some of them:

Spotify, Apple Music, iTunes, Instagram/Facebook, TikTok/Resso, YouTube Music, Amazon, Soundtrack by Twitch, Pandora, Deezer, Tidal, iHeartRadio, Claro Música, Boomplay, Anghami, KKBox, NetEase, Tencent, Triller, Yandex Music, MediaNet

To make it easier to upload your music to all platforms at once instead of one by one, you can use a digital distribution service. This allows you to manage your music from a central dashboard and for revenue for online streaming and purchasing to be collected on your behalf. You only need one, but they do offer slightly different prices and services, so you'll likely want to compare them.

Here are some examples of digital distribution services you could use:

- DistroKid (`https://distrokid.com/`)
- LANDR (`https://www.landr.com/`)
- CD Baby (`https://cdbaby.com/`)
- TuneCore (`https://www.tunecore.com/`)
- Ditto Music (`https://www.dittomusic.com/`)
- Loudr (`https://www.crunchbase.com/organization/loudr`)
- Record Union (`https://www.recordunion.com/`)
- ReverbNation (`https://www.reverbnation.com/`)
- Symphonic (`https://symphonicdistribution.com/`)
- iMusician (`https://imusician.pro/en/`)

> **Note:**
> If you choose to use DistroKid as your digital distribution provider service, the following link provides you with a discount on your first year: `https://distrokid.com/vip/seven/701180`.

If you can, try to negotiate to keep the rights to your songs. Collecting royalties on your music is an additional source of revenue available to composers.

Summary

In this chapter, we learned about the business of composing music for clients. We learned about how to land a job creating music for clients to jumpstart your composing career. We discussed advice for how to come across as professional so that clients take you seriously, and we learned how to prepare for client meetings so that you use your client's time effectively. We learned how to plan out film scores so that you can schedule properly, how to collaborate with others when sharing project files, and how to use Splice for version control. Finally, we discussed how to collect royalties for your music.

In the next chapter, we'll learn how to use a digital audio workstation so that you can get started composing music.

Part 2: Composing Tools and Techniques

In this section, you will learn how to navigate the FL Studio workspace. You will learn practical music theory for composers and how to apply it. You will also learn how to create orchestral music using FL Studio.

We will cover the following chapters in this section:

- *Chapter 2, Navigating Through the Key Features of FL Studio*
- *Chapter 3, Designing Music with Themes, Leitmotifs, and Scales*
- *Chapter 4, Orchestral MIDI Composing*

2
Navigating Through the Key Features of FL Studio

In this chapter, we will discuss the main features of the digital audio workstation FL Studio. We'll discuss what FL Studio is, how to get it, and take an introductory look at the core tools of it. Specifically, we'll discuss how to use the Channel rack, the Piano roll, the Playlist, the Browser, and the Mixer. Finally, we'll learn how to record audio and how to export music.

We will cover the following topics in this chapter:

- What is FL Studio?
- FL Studio's core tools: the Channel rack, the Piano roll, the Playlist, the Browser, and the Mixer
- Recording audio
- Exporting music

What is FL Studio?

FL Studio is one of the world's leading digital audio workstations. It's a software suite that lets you do pretty much anything you ever wanted to do while creating music. You can use FL Studio for all of your composing needs. You can play instrument plugins, record audio, create chord progressions, mix music, and score videos all within this software. We will be using FL Studio to compose music throughout this book.

Get FL Studio

You can download a trial version of FL Studio for free. The trial version lets you try out all the plugins to see what they can do. You can use all of the tools in FL Studio but won't let you reopen saved projects until you purchase a version.

You can download FL Studio from the Image Line website: `https://www.image-line.com/`:

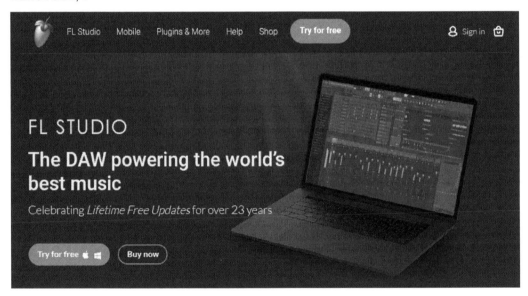

Figure 2.1 – The FL Studio website

There are several version tiers of FL Studio available for purchase. Here's a breakdown of the versions so that you can make sure you are getting the features you need:

- The **Fruity Edition** is the cheapest. It includes all the basic features, such as access to the playlist, the Channel rack, the Piano roll, the Browser, and the Mixer. It includes the Autogun, BassDrum, BeepMap, Drumpad, FLEX, Fruit Kick, Fruity DX10, Groove Machine Synth, Distructor, and MiniSynth plugins, but it does not include audio recording.

- The **Producer Edition** includes all features in the Fruity Edition, plus audio recording and post-production tools. If you want to record audio, you will need this version or higher. This version also includes the Edison, Slicex, Sytrus, Maximus, Vocodex, and SynthMaker plugins.

- The **Signature Bundle** includes everything in the Producer Edition, plus Fruity Video Player, the DirectWave sampler, Harmless, NewTone, Pitcher, Gross Beat, Vintage Chorus, and the Hardcore guitar effects suite. Fruity Video Player allows you to see videos in sync with your music, which is handy for film composers. We will discuss how to use Fruity Video Player to score videos in *Chapter 5, Creating Sheet Music with MuseScore, Scoring with Fruity Video Player, and Diegetic Music.*

- The **All Plugins Bundle** includes all possible plugins and features created by Image Line at the time of purchase, including a large selection of instruments and effects.

There are a lot more features included in each edition. For a full comparison of product versions, visit `https://www.image-line.com/fl-studio/compare-editions/`.

FL Studio provides lifetime free updates. This helps to ensure that you're always using the latest and greatest features available. Whenever the FL Studio team comes out with new software plugins, you can get them instantly just by updating FL Studio. Over the years, FL Studio has made some major advancements, and the lifetime updates add up over time to be really important.

The official FL Studio YouTube channel, *Image-Line* (`https://www.youtube.com/user/imageline`), keeps you up to date with new FL Studio features by posting every software update. Whenever FL Studio releases new features, they release a tutorial video, overviewing what's new.

Now that we know what FL Studio is, let's jump in and start using the tools.

FL Studio core tools

Tools in FL Studio can only be really understood once you start using them. This is a book about composing techniques, so instead of listing every control and feature, we'll just focus on the need-to-know features and then get to the fun stuff – composing. In this chapter, we will cover the basics for beginners. We'll load an instrument into the Channel rack, create a simple melody in the Piano roll, add it to the Playlist, route it to the Mixer, and export it from FL Studio.

At the top of FL Studio, you'll find the menu panel and the player. The menu panel contains the **FILE** navigation dropdown for creating, saving, opening, and exporting projects. Below **FILE**, you'll see text describing the name of whatever button your mouse cursor hovers over, as well as a list of keyboard shortcuts for using the control. If you're ever wondering what a plugin or control is called, it will be described here. The following screenshot shows the menu panel and the player:

Figure 2.2 – FILE

In the preceding screenshot, you'll see a button with **PAT** and **SONG**. Left-clicking allows you to toggle between options, switching between playing patterns and songs. Think of a pattern as a group of melodies played by instruments. Songs are bigger than patterns; they consist of multiple music patterns, as well as samples and automation.

To the right of the **PAT** and **SONG** buttons are the Play and Stop buttons, which will play your music. Alternatively, you can press the spacebar to start and stop playing audio.

There are five main tool sections in FL Studio, accessible by left-clicking the following buttons:

Figure 2.3 – Tools

The preceding screenshot lists, from left to right, the Playlist, the Piano roll, the Channel rack, the Mixer, and the Browser. In order to compose successfully with FL Studio, you will need to understand at least the basics of each of these. The following diagram shows how the tools relate to each other:

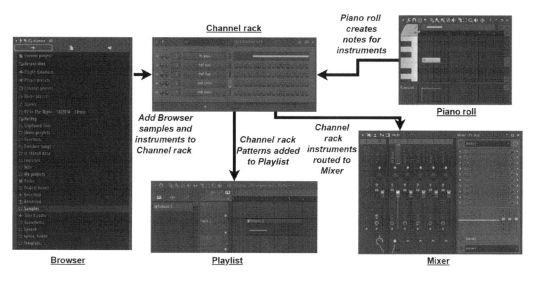

Figure 2.4 – FL Studio tools

These tools connect to each other as follows:

- The Browser helps with file navigation. Here, you can grab sound samples and navigate through your folders.

- The Channel rack displays all the instruments, samples, and automation used in your project. This is where you can add new instruments to be used.

- The Piano roll is where you create note melodies for any instrument that you've loaded into the Channel rack.

- The Playlist contains all the patterns, samples, and automation used in your song. This is the dashboard showing all your sounds.

- The Mixer is where you add effects to your sounds. You can route instruments and sounds from the Channel rack to the Mixer and then can edit the sounds in the Mixer.

Don't worry if some of this goes over your head at first; it's a little confusing to understand by short descriptions alone. We will discuss each of these in this chapter.

Logically, the first thing you do when you are creating a song is pick an instrument to create music with. This is done using the Channel rack tool.

The Channel rack

The **Channel rack** tool holds all of your instruments, samples, and automations, and allows you to navigate between them. Whenever you want to see what instruments you've added to your project, this is the tool that you will be using. Open up the Channel rack by left-clicking on the **Channel rack** icon:

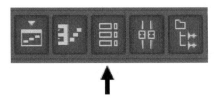

Figure 2.5 – The Channel rack icon

When you open the Channel rack, you'll see something similar to the following:

Figure 2.6 – The Channel rack

At the top-left corner of the Channel rack, you'll see the **Channel Options** drop-down arrow. Left-click **Channel Options | Add one**, and you'll see a list of all the instrument plugins available for you. Alternatively, you can right-click on any instrument in the Channel rack to see the same options:

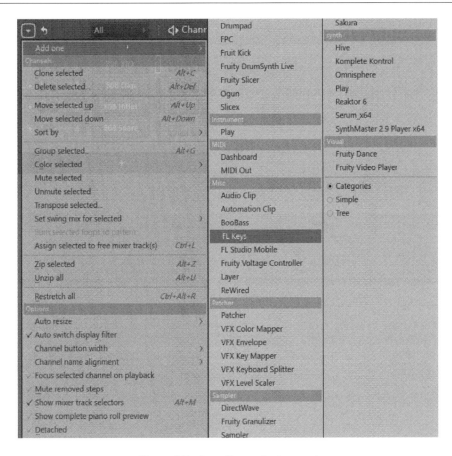

Figure 2.7 – Inserting an instrument

From the panel, you can left-click on any instrument, and it will be added to the Channel rack. I encourage you to explore the instruments available at your leisure. For now, we'll select the FL Keys instrument:

Figure 2.8 – FL Keys

The instrument plugin will open. If you press down on keyboard letters or a connected **Musical Instrument Digital Interface** (**MIDI**) keyboard, you will be able to hear the instrument notes playing.

If dealing with percussion samples, you can create instrument notes directly on the Channel rack by left-clicking on the note buttons in the Channel rack, as shown in the following screenshot:

Figure 2.9 – Channel rack notes

When you play the pattern, you will be able to hear the instruments playing notes.

On the left-hand side of the Channel rack, you can see the **Mute/Solo** buttons, and the **Channel Panning**, **Channel Volume**, and **Target Mixer Track** controls, as shown in the following screenshot:

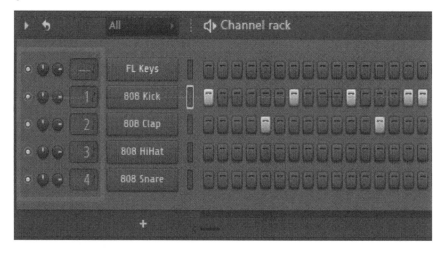

Figure 2.10 – Mute, Pan, Volume, and Mixer Track

The **Mute/Solo** buttons enable you to turn on and off individual instruments. For example, if you hold down *Ctrl* + left-click on the **Mute/Solo** button, it will mute all other instruments. This helps to isolate individual sounds, making it easier to hear one at a time. To turn on all the instruments again, hold down *Ctrl* + left-click on the **Mute/Solo** button a second time.

The **Channel Panning** knob allows you to hear what the audio sounds like coming from the left or right speaker. **Target Mixer Track** shows you which mixer track the instrument is currently routed to. We'll come back to this later in this chapter.

Here are some useful Channel rack shortcuts:

- **Clone channel**: *Alt* + *C*
- **Delete channel**: *Alt* + *Del*
- **Re-order channels**: *Alt* + up/down
- **Transpose channel steps**: *Ctrl* + *Shift* + left/right
- **Zip channels**: *Alt* + *Z*
- **Filter groups**: *Alt* + *G*

Whenever you look at the Channel rack, you'll see all the instruments used in your project. If notes are added to one or more instruments in a pattern, you'll see this show up in the Channel rack.

Now that we've learned how to use the Channel rack, let's learn how to add music notes to an instrument using the Piano roll.

Using the Piano roll

The **Piano roll** is where you compose chord melodies and progressions. This is where all the magic happens for composers. We will come back to the Piano roll again and again throughout this book.

Let's add some notes for our instrument to play. Right-click on the instrument you want to compose notes for in the Channel rack and choose the **Piano roll** option. In the following screenshot, you can see that I'm opening **FL Keys** in the Piano roll:

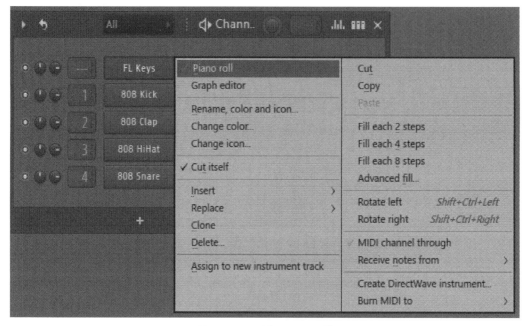

Figure 2.11 – The Piano roll

Alternatively, you can open the Piano roll by selecting the **Piano roll** icon:

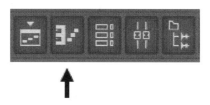

Figure 2.12 – The Piano roll icon

The Piano roll tool will open, and you'll see the Piano roll. At the top of the screen, you'll see the words **Piano roll**, followed by the instrument currently selected. Clicking the text allows you to navigate between instruments, as shown in the following screenshot:

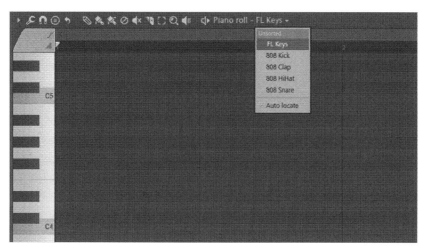

Figure 2.13 – Piano roll instrument navigation

The Piano roll looks like a piano with a timeline from left to right. On the left, you'll see black and white rectangular boxes to represent piano keys/note pitches. To the right of the piano notes, you'll see a grid of blue boxes in what resembles a spreadsheet table. These boxes indicate a position in time. By adding notes into the grid, you are telling the instrument to play specific note pitches at specific times.

To add notes, first check whether the Draw tool is enabled, which is the symbol that looks like a pencil at the top of the Piano roll. Most of the time, you'll want the Draw tool to be enabled. Left-click anywhere in the grid to add some notes. A rectangle will appear in the grid, indicating that a note was added, as shown in the following screenshot:

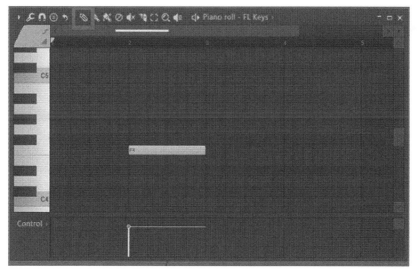

Figure 2.14 – The Draw tool

By changing the note pitches over time, you'll create melodies. By adding multiple notes playing at the same time, you'll construct chords. If you now play your pattern by pressing Spacebar, you will be able to hear the Piano roll play your musical notes.

Now that we've learned how to add notes, let's learn how to manipulate them.

Deleting notes

If you have the Draw tool selected, you can delete notes by right-clicking in the Piano roll and dragging over the notes that you want to delete. Alternatively, you can enable the Delete tool symbol that is to the right of the Draw tool at the top of the Piano roll.

Muting notes (ghost notes)

I find myself muting and unmuting notes on a regular basis. Muting notes means that you can visually see the note in the Piano roll, but it makes no sound when the pattern is played. These are often called **ghost notes**, which just means notes that are muted. Ghost notes help us see what notes can be used when trying to figure out which ones to add next.

You can mute notes by double right-clicking on an empty space in the Piano roll and then dragging over the ones that you want to mute. In the following screenshot, the top two notes are muted (the ghost notes):

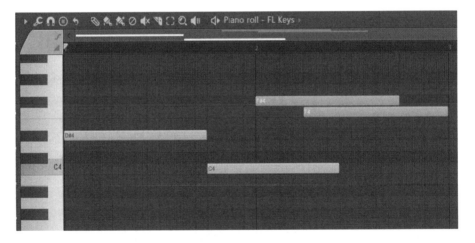

Figure 2.15 – Ghost notes

Ghost notes are useful when you want to experiment with turning notes on and off. It retains the placement positioning of the notes so that you can easily reenable them when needed.

You can select a group of notes at once and then mute or unmute them. You can select multiple notes at once by holding down *Ctrl + Shift* and dragging over the notes that you want to select, and then muting the notes with the *Alt + M* shortcut. You can unmute selected notes with the *Ctrl + Shift + M* shortcut.

Alternatively, you can mute notes using the Mute tool icon at the top of the Piano roll.

Splitting notes

Sometimes, you'll want to break a note into pieces. You can chop notes in half using the right *Alt* + right *Shift* shortcut and dragging over the note where you want to chop the note. Alternatively, you can chop notes in half by using the splitting tool at the top of the Piano roll.

We've learned the basics of how to use the Piano roll. We'll cover lots of composing techniques in the Piano roll in detail in *Chapter 3, Designing Music with Themes, Leitmotifs, and Scales*, and *Chapter 4, Orchestral MIDI Composing*.

Next, let's learn about the Playlist.

The Playlist

The **Playlist** is where you arrange the timing of all elements for your song. It holds patterns, Audio Clips, and the automation of effects.

Once you've created some notes in the Piano roll, it means that you've added notes to a single pattern. Now, it's time to add your pattern to the Playlist. Open the Playlist by selecting the **Playlist** icon:

Figure 2.16 – The Playlist icon

Once selected, the Playlist will open, as shown in the following screenshot:

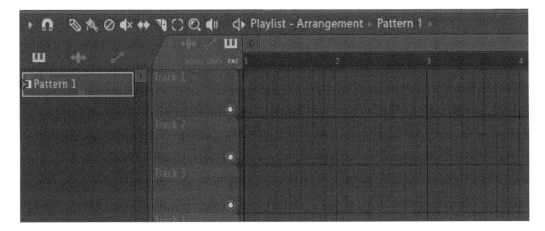

Figure 2.17 – The Playlist

If you left-click on the Playlist, you will be able to add a selected pattern to it.

In the following screenshot, the pattern selected is **Pattern 1**, as indicated by the text **Playlist - Arrangement > Pattern 1 >**, as shown at the top of the Playlist. This is the pattern you just created some notes for. By left-clicking on the Playlist, the pattern will be added at the selected position, as shown in the following screenshot:

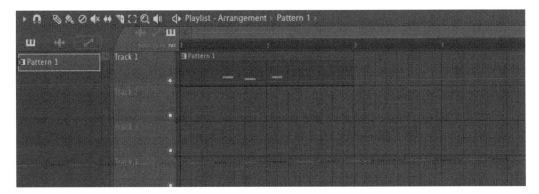

Figure 2.18 – Adding a pattern to the Playlist

If you want to add a different pattern, you can either select the **Current clip source** button or the pattern selector and choose your desired pattern, as indicated in the following screenshot:

Figure 2.19 – Changing a pattern in the Playlist

In the preceding screenshot, you can see that I have two patterns available to be added. One of them is called **Pattern 1**, and the other is called **Pattern 2**. You can rename them for visual convenience.

Here are some essential keyboard shortcuts to help speed up composing. Once you've committed these shortcuts to muscle memory, you'll find using the Piano roll and the Playlist enjoyable:

- **Delete notes**: Right-click on the note
- **Duplicate notes**: *Ctrl* + *B*
- **Alternative duplicate method**: Left *Shift* + click and drag
- **Mute/unmute**: Double-right-click and drag over the sound clip
- **Split clip**: Right *Alt* + right *Shift* + left-click
- **Drag a clip while ignoring tempo**: *Alt* + left-click and drag
- **Select clip**: *Ctrl* + right-click
- **Select multiple clips**: *Ctrl* + *Shift* + left-click
- **Select all**: *Ctrl* + *A*
- **Zoom to full view**: *Ctrl* + right-click
- **Zoom in**: *Ctrl* + scroll with the mouse wheel

These all complement the more general shortcuts:

- **Undo**: *Ctrl + Z*
- **Redo**: *Ctrl + Alt + Z*
- **Copy**: *Ctrl + C*
- **Paste**: *Ctrl + V*

We've now learned how to add music patterns to the Playlist. Next, let's understand how patterns are related to songs.

Understanding patterns versus songs

Beginners may find it difficult to understand why their music isn't playing when they try to play it. This is usually due to not understanding the concepts of patterns and songs and getting them mixed up. Let's take a quick moment to make sure we understand how to navigate between patterns and songs.

The following screenshot shows the buttons you use to toggle between **PAT** and **SONG**:

Figure 2.20 – PAT versus SONG

If you have **PAT** selected, you will hear the chosen pattern playing. If **SONG** is selected, you will hear all the audio playing in the Playlist. So, if you aren't hearing the entire song, it's likely because you have a specific pattern selected. In other words, when you want to compose for a specific group of instruments, you want to have **PAT** selected. The pattern then gets added to the Playlist. When you want to hear the whole song, you'll want to have **SONG** selected, which will play everything in the Playlist.

Once you've chosen **PAT**, this will enable you to listen to individual patterns. You can navigate between selected patterns in two ways. The easiest way is to find the desired playlist pattern to the left of the Playlist and left-click to select it, as shown in the following screenshot:

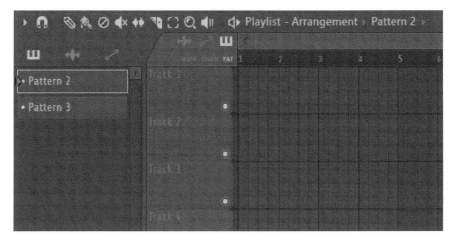

Figure 2.21 – Selecting a pattern

Another approach is to select the **Pattern** options dropdown, as shown in the following screenshot:

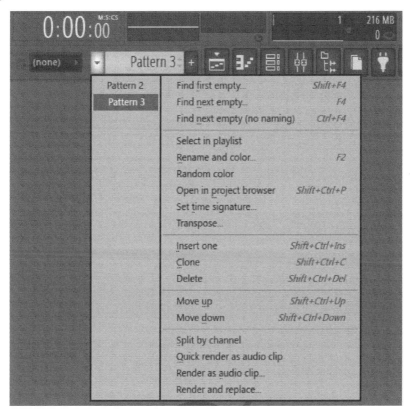

Figure 2.22 – Pattern options

You now know how to navigate the Playlist and add patterns to it. So far, we've learned how to load an instrument in the Channel rack, add music pattern notes for the instrument to play, and add music patterns to the Playlist. Next, let's learn about the Mixer.

The Mixer

The Mixer is where you apply audio effects onto sounds and balance the volume of sounds relative to one another. It's where all your sounds get sent when you want to add effects to enhance them.

Before you can mix and add effects to your instruments, you need to connect your instruments to mixer track channels. Let's route our instruments to the Mixer. There are a few ways to route an instrument from the Channel rack to the Mixer. My preferred method is to select the instrument by left-clicking the select button directly to the right of the instrument name, and then pressing the *Ctrl + Shift + l* keyboard shortcut:

Figure 2.23 – Selecting an instrument

This will route the instrument, name, and assigned instrument color of all selected tracks to the Mixer. If you want to route just a single instrument, you can also use *Ctrl + l*.

Another method to route instruments to the Mixer is to right-click on the instrument and select the **Assign to new instrument track** option, as shown in the following screenshot:

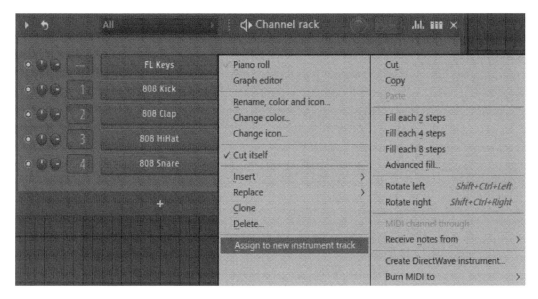

Figure 2.24 – Assigning to a new instrument track

Another method is to hover your mouse cursor over the **Target Mixer Track** button and scroll with the mouse wheel, or drag it up and down. This will assign a mixer track value for the instrument, as shown in the following screenshot:

Figure 2.25 – Target Mixer Track

After routing your instruments from the Channel rack to the router, you can open up the Mixer by left-clicking on the Mixer icon, as shown in the following screenshot:

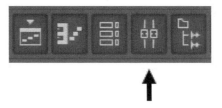

Figure 2.26 – The Mixer icon

The mixer will open up, and you will see a screen similar to the following:

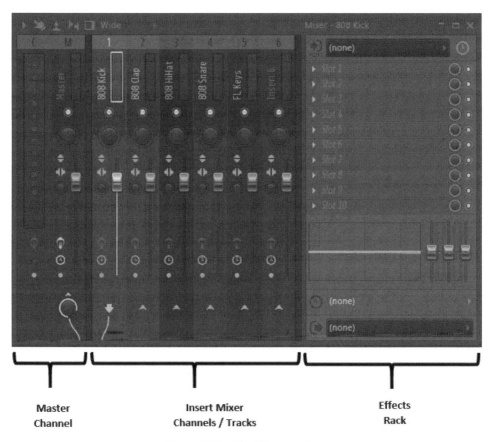

Figure 2.27 – The Mixer sections

The Mixer is divided up into three main sections:

- The insert mixer channels/tracks

- The effects rack

- The master channel

We use the names *track* or *channel* interchangeably throughout this book, as they mean the same thing.

The **insert mixer tracks** section lists the name of the instrument routed to it, which you can select by left-clicking. Each channel contains a volume knob that can be dragged up or down to adjust the volume of the instrument, as well as the panning knob to control whether you hear audio from the right or left speaker.

Once you have left-clicked on a channel, you can now apply effects to a sound by left-clicking on an empty slot in the effects rack. The following screenshot shows an example of adding an effect to a mixer track:

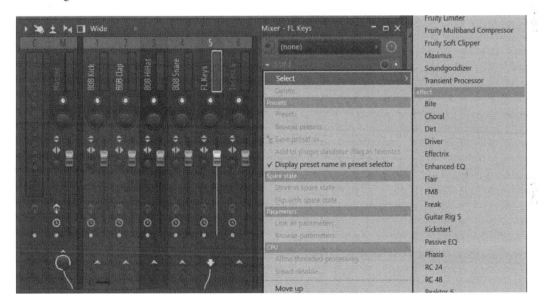

Figure 2.28 – The effects rack

A list of effects will appear, which you can left-click to add. You can add effects such as delay, compression, equalization, and reverb.

The master channel section is where all your audio from the Mixer eventually gets routed to. Audio exiting the master channel is the final outputted sound that you export.

Next, let's learn about the Browser tool.

The Browser

The Browser is mainly used to help you to navigate through the samples and files that you want to use in your project. You can open the Browser by clicking the **Browser** icon:

Figure 2.29 – The Browser icon

Inside the Browser, you'll see a series of folders. If you left-click on the **Packs** folder and then the **Legacy** folder, you'll see a list of samples that you can use:

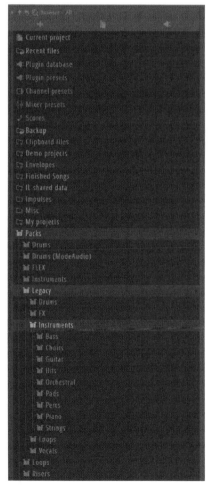

Figure 2.30 – Browser instruments

These folders contain a combination of sound samples and instruments. You can then right-click on the instrument/sample and route it to your desired location, such as the Channel rack. Alternatively, you can left-click and drag from the Browser into the Playlist. The following screenshot shows an example of right-clicking on a sample and routing it to the Channel rack:

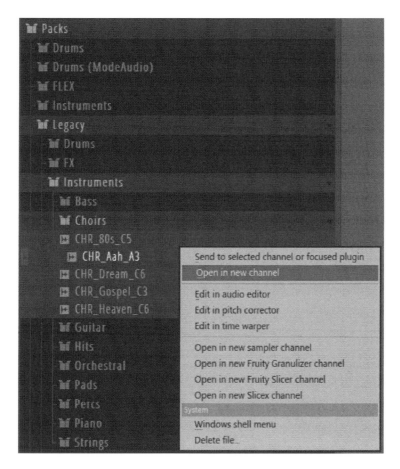

Figure 2.31 – Using samples

In the preceding screenshot, you can see several menu options appearing when you right-click on a sample in the Browser. The **Open in new Channel** option will send the sample straight to the Channel rack.

One cool thing about samples is that you can swap them with each other with ease. To do so, select the desired sample in the Playlist or the Channel rack. Then, in the Browser, press the scroll button on your mouse (the middle mouse button) while clicking on the sample you want to replace. This will swap the sample clips. I use this shortcut quite often.

Another very cool browser feature is the **Scores** folder. The **Scores** folder contains MIDI note suggestions. You can drag MIDI files from this folder onto instruments in the Channel rack. This will populate the instrument with notes, as shown in the following screenshot:

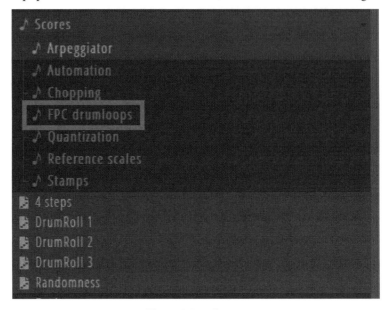

Figure 2.32 – Scores

For example, the **FPC drumloops** folder contains drumbeat MIDI data that you can use for the FPC instrument or any other drum kit instrument.

So far, we've learned how to use the core tools of FL Studio. We learned how to use the Channel rack, the Piano roll, the Playlist, the Mixer, and the Browser. Next, let's learn how to record audio in FL Studio.

Recording audio

In order to record live sounds in FL Studio, you will need the Producer Edition of FL Studio or higher.

When recording audio in FL Studio, you will need to have a microphone connected to your computer. When you have the microphone connected, open up the Mixer, select an empty mixer track by left-clicking, and then select the audio input source and choose your microphone. The following screenshot shows how to select a microphone; in my case, the microphone name is **ln 1 - ln 2** (yours will have a different name):

Figure 2.33 – Selecting a microphone

Once you've chosen your microphone, you are now ready to record audio. If you look at the Mixer, you'll notice a little red indicator on a selected mixer track, as shown in the following screenshot:

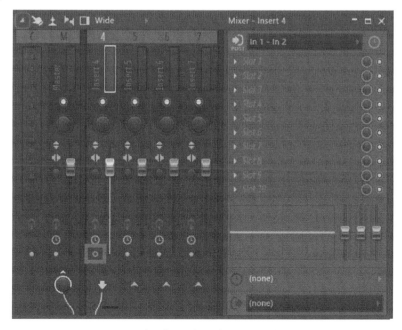

Figure 2.34 – The channel ready to record audio input

This red light indicates that recorded audio will be sent to that selected mixer track. Any effects on the track will also be applied to the audio while recording. You can record on multiple mixer tracks at the same time if desired. In general, it's a good practice to record raw audio and then apply effects later on, but you do have the option of applying effects while recording, which is useful if you want to see how pitch-correction effects such as autotune might sound.

We've got our mixer set up. Now, let's record. To record audio, left-click on the **Record** (**automation, score**) button as shown in the following screenshot:

Figure 2.35 – The Record button

The recording window will appear. You can then select one of the recording options available. You can choose any of the options to record, but for this example, we will choose the **Audio, into the playlist as an audio clip** option:

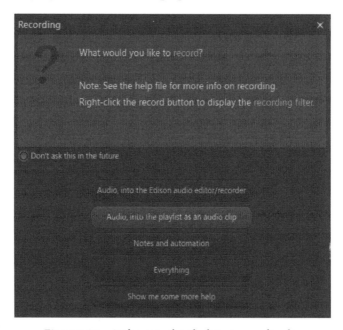

Figure 2.36 – Audio, into the playlist as an audio clip

Your playlist song will begin playing. Any audio you record now will play in time with the Playlist music, as shown in the following screenshot:

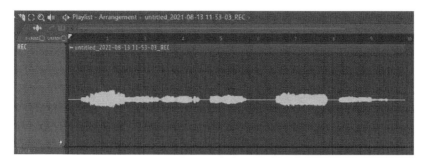

Figure 2.37 – Audio recorded in the Playlist

To record just your audio input without hearing the rest of the music from the Playlist in the background of the recording, you will need headphones connected to your computer. Otherwise, you will record the sound coming out of your speakers back into FL Studio. Always record audio wearing headphones.

Congratulations! You just learned how to record audio. Next, let's learn how to export our music composition.

Exporting music

Let's learn how to export our music from FL Studio. The master channel in the Mixer, as shown in the following screenshot, contains the final audio that will be exported:

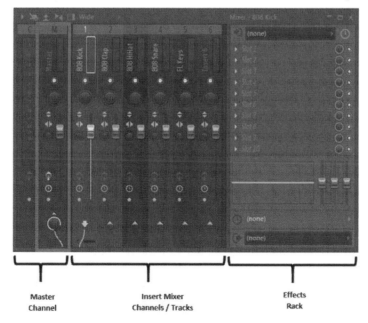

Figure 2.38 – The master channel

To export the song, go to **FILE | Export | Wave file**:

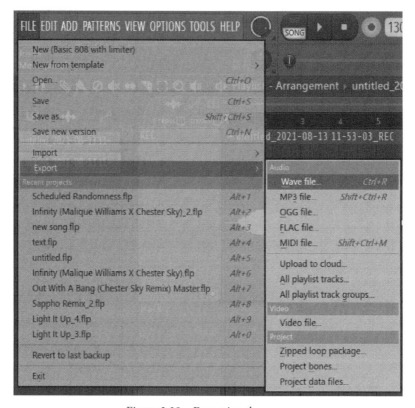

Figure 2.39 – Exporting the song

After selecting **Wave file**, you will be prompted to choose where to save your audio file. Then, you'll see a window with song exporting controls, as shown in the following screenshot:

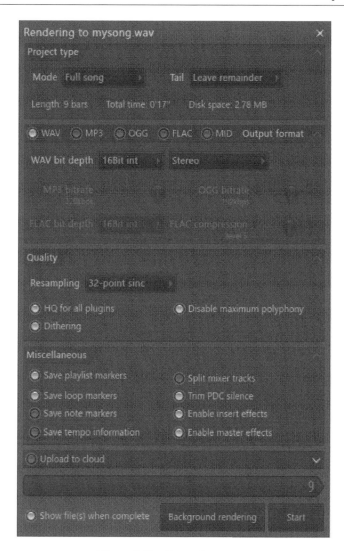

Figure 2.40 – Exporting a song

The simplest way to export your song is to make sure that **Mode** is set to **Full Song**. Then, select **WAV** or **MP3**, and click **Start**. This will export your song so that you can listen to your music outside of FL Studio. Congratulations! You've exported your song.

In case you're curious, here's a breakdown of the export settings in detail. In the **Project type** options, you can choose to export your full song or just a single pattern.

The **Tail** option has the following three choices to pick from:

- **Cut remainder** abruptly ends the song the moment the sound and samples stop playing.

- **Leave remainder** allows synthesizers to naturally decay to silence at the end of your song. This is usually the choice you'll want in most scenarios.

- **Wrap remainder** takes any decay that appears at the end of your song and places it at the start of your song. This is useful in circumstances where you are creating a loop and want the sound to repeat.

Underneath, you can see the song length, the total elapsed time of the song, and the size of the file the exported song will create.

You can choose between several outputted format types. You can choose to export as a **WAV** or **FLAC**, which are lossless formats that don't degrade in audio quality. For final versions of audio, you will likely want to export using the **WAV** format. Bit depth is the resolution you can choose to output. The options available are as follows:

- **16-bit**, the standard for CD quality

- **24-bit**, recommended for streaming

- **32-bit**, for sound archive size

You can usually select 16-bit, as you likely won't be able to tell the difference between higher-bit file sizes in most cases.

FLAC uses data compression to reduce the file size; however, the sound will be identical to a **WAV** file. You can then increase the **FLAC** compression, which will make the file size smaller, but it still won't affect the sound quality; it will just take a little longer to export.

MP3 and **OGG** are formats that will lose audio quality when exporting. They throw away data while maintaining audio sound. **MP3 bitrate** determines the audio quality; a higher bitrate allows a higher quality sound.

The **MID** format allows you to export your project as MIDI data, assuming that you created MIDI data in your project.

You also have the option of selecting to output in **Stereo** or **Mono**. This refers to whether you want to allow differences in sound coming from the left and right speakers or if you want the sound to be identical. You'll usually want to leave this as stereo.

The **Quality** section refers to dithering. Essentially, it can make it seem like your music is slightly higher resolution than it actually is for the chosen file size.

Under **Miscellaneous**, you'll want to make sure that the **Enable insert effects** and **Enable master effects** options are selected so that your mixer effects are applied. Leave **Trim PDC silence** on; this adds any necessary silence to the beginning of your track to ensure that the sounds are in sync.

The **Split mixer tracks** option is what you'll use if you want to export a different sound file for each mixer track. You do this if you want to send your song to a third party for mixing or mastering. Doing this will result in a different audio file for every insert mixer track. These files are known as **audio stems**. If you are collaborating with another musician who isn't using FL Studio, you will need to send the music stems to them so that they can manipulate your audio samples. We will cover splitting mixer tracks more in *Chapter 7, Creating Interactive Music for Video Games with Wwise*.

Congratulations! You've just created your first song in FL Studio. We've now covered the basics of the tools that FL Studio offers. It's the barebones with just enough to get you started because we need to move on to learn about composing techniques. If you want to master FL Studio and explore the features in detail, I give a comprehensive breakdown in the book *The Music Producer's Ultimate Guide to FL Studio 20, Packt Publishing*: `https://www.amazon.ca/Music-Producers-Ultimate-Guide-Studio/dp/1800565321`.

Summary

In this chapter, we learned the essentials of FL Studio. We learned how to add instruments with the Channel rack, how to add notes so that we can create melodies using the Piano roll, and how to add music patterns to the Playlist so that we can arrange your melodies. We learned how to add effects to our music using the Mixer, how to add samples and MIDI data using the Browser, and how to record audio. Finally, we learned how to export our music from FL Studio.

In the next chapter, we'll learn useful music theory for composing.

3
Designing Music with Themes, Leitmotifs, and Scales

In this chapter, we discuss music theory for composers. We will give a foundational background for how to apply music theory for film and game composing. We will discuss how the concepts of motifs, themes, and leitmotifs can be used to come up with musical ideas. We will discuss what scales are and how to use them. We will use scales to explain what modes are and how to use them. Finally, these concepts will allow us to use the Circle of Fifths chord wheel tool to show how scales relate to each other and how to smoothly transition from one music key to another within a song.

We will cover the following topics in this chapter:

- Toolkit of the composer
- Understanding and using themes, motifs, and leitmotifs
- Understanding scales

- Understanding and using modes
- Understanding sharps and flats
- Using the Circle of Fifths chord wheel

Toolkit of the composer

When you sit down to compose (usually at a piano and computer), you're faced with a blank canvas. At least that's how it's depicted in movies. It looks like there's nothing, and you have to invent. From an outsider's perspective, it seems like the music just pours out of you. That's the romantic fairytale way of thinking about composing music.

Music bursting out of you sounds lovely but isn't very reliable if you need to create music consistently on demand. Where does music come from? The notes we play aren't random. Certain note combinations and melodies sometimes sound really good together. It seems like sometimes all the notes flow and support each other. How does this come about? There must be some kind of relationship between note combinations that allow this to happen.

You've been given a film composing assignment. You've seen the story you need to create music for. How do you start? How can you make music that meets your desired style and stays consistent throughout? What frameworks are there to help guide the process? This chapter aims to answer all these questions.

When you actually get to the composing task, it can be a very technical art. You can compare composing to how a carpenter creates a sculpture out of wood. Yes, you need an idea of what you want to make before you sculpt, but the creation is hugely shaped by the tools you have available. The more mastery you have of your tools, the more opportunities you'll find. Understanding how to use your tools and what the bigger picture is behind the tools go hand in hand.

There are lots of tools at the composer's disposal and we will explore many throughout this book. In order to make the most of software tools, you need to have a conceptual understanding of music. In this chapter, we'll focus on the big-picture theory to figure out what you're composing. Then, in later chapters, we'll look at the tools to execute your vision. By the end of this chapter, you'll understand how music theory can be applied to compose music.

Themes, motifs, and leitmotifs

Before you begin composing, we need to come up with some parameters to compose around. Themes, motifs, and leitmotifs are tools for coming up with musical ideas. They can help us to understand the meaning of scenes and define the qualities we want our music to have.

If you've taken a writing or film critiquing course, you may already be familiar with the terms themes, motifs, and leitmotifs. However, there could be many interpretations of these terms depending on who is teaching, and these terms are usually not used in a musical context. In the context of our discussion, we'll define these terms as follows:

Motif

A **motif** is a fragmentary musical idea that cannot represent something concrete in a narrative. It's a group or phrase of notes that convey an idea. It's the smallest amount of music you can make meaningful. As you replay this group of notes at different points throughout the narrative, the motif will come to mean different things. The important part is that you keep coming back to this musical idea throughout the story. If you keep expanding this musical idea and extending it, it can evolve into a musical theme.

As an example of a motif, in the 1960 film *Psycho*, directed by Alfred Hitchcock, when the shower murder scene occurs, we hear the screeching of violins. It's a high-pitch, clashing, dissonant sound that is unpleasant and jarring. This sound becomes associated with the sound of murder.

Theme

A **theme** is a complete musical idea that can represent something concrete in a narrative, but it doesn't have to. It's a recognizable melody, upon which part or all of the composition is based. When you hear a musical theme, you know the song is referring to a specific story.

Whenever you watch a TV show, the show has a theme song. The song becomes associated with the show. The theme is often thought of as a sound that sums up the idea of the show.

In many live theater operas and stage shows, a live band plays music before the show begins. At this point, they'll play several musical themes for the show. It's often a mashup compilation of several musical pieces played throughout.

How do motifs compare to themes?

Motifs are small ideas that develop into a bigger theme. Motifs are the recurrent image, idea, or symbol that develops or explains a theme, whereas a theme is a central idea or message. A motif does not represent anything on its own. It's a small, short musical idea. The meaning of the motif depends on the visual that accompanies it. A theme is more used for a summary collection of visuals.

Leitmotif

A **leitmotif** is a fragmentary musical idea that must represent something concrete in a narrative.

The composer Wilhelm Richard Wagner is often credited with coming up with the idea of leitmotifs. He created operas and wanted everything in the opera to have meaning behind it. Every costume, every action, all the characters on the stage: they had to each have their own individual meaning.

We can assign different characters, actions, places, and events their own musical idea.

There's a great example of a leitmotif in the 1977 movie *Close Encounters of the Third Kind*, directed by Steven Spielberg. If you haven't seen it yet, the following will be a spoiler. If you haven't already seen the movie, you may want to watch it and then come back.

In the film *Close Encounters of the Third Kind*, humans and aliens try to communicate with each other but don't understand each other. The method of communication they end up using is a 5-note musical phrase. The 5-note melody is repeated constantly throughout the movie with different sounds and instruments, but you don't quite understand why until much later on. In the story's climax, we discover that the music is how humans and aliens can talk to each other. In this film example, the 5-note musical phrase is a leitmotif. It has a specific concrete meaning, and that meaning is the word *hello*.

How to use motifs, themes, and leitmotifs

When you're looking through your video footage and trying to figure out what music needs to be composed, one approach is to come up with a list of all the central characters, places, events, and other noteworthy items important to the plot. Then, try to come up with music motifs and leitmotifs that reflect those items. Once you've come up with the initial motifs and leitmotifs, you can expand on the idea until you have a full song.

Let's discuss an example. In the films *Star Wars*, *The Empire Strikes Back*, and *Return of the Jedi*, directed by George Lucas, every time you see the character Darth Vader, there's a specific song that plays. This song is *The Imperial March*, more commonly known as Darth Vader's theme. You associate the sound with Darth Vader throughout the film. Darth Vader's theme is so tied together with the character, it's hard to imagine that at one point there was no music. We just take it for granted that that music plays at the same time as the character appears.

Imagine we'd never heard the music to be used for Darth Vader. Let's think about the music for Darth Vader's theme and try to reverse engineer how composer John Williams might have come up with the music.

Pretend you were watching *Star Wars* on mute and saw Darth Vader on video for the first time. What information do you have to work with when trying to come up with musical ideas?

By looking at scenes where Darth Vader appears, we learn a few things. Vader is the villain of the movie. He's bad, strong, powerful, and commands an army. When he walks into a room, he commands the attention of everyone around him. He's always wearing black full-body armor. If you unmute and listen, when he speaks, he has a deep masculine voice that sounds menacing.

All we've done is look at the physical appearance of the character and we already have a lot of information to start coming up with music. John Williams chose to make Vader's theme in the style of a march. If we want to reinforce the physical appearance of the character as being some form of military commander, then music in the rhythm of a military march is a logical choice. If we want to articulate the idea of power, then we'll likely want to use instruments that can support that feeling. John Williams ended up using lots of low bass string notes, lots of percussion, and big brass instruments.

Thinking about leitmotifs can help you to choose what sounds and instruments you might want to use. You can look at the characters, places, events, or other significant items and see what meaning they have. Then, try to figure out what sounds go well to convey that meaning.

We've learned about motifs, themes, and leitmotifs and how they can be used to come up with musical ideas. Next, let's learn about scales.

Understanding scales

Try to learn any melodic instrument and sooner or later you'll learn about scales. If you're trying to compose songs, an understanding of scales is required.

When talking about scales, most music books dive straight into music notation, ask you to memorize scales, and leave you with a book of pages you'll likely never read. I've seen many of these books and lectures and found most of them completely forgettable. We're going to try another approach to help you see why we use scales and how to apply them. This will help you to understand music theory rather than memorize it. In fact, you don't have to memorize much at all; software can do almost all the work for you.

In this chapter, we'll explore answers to the following questions: what are scales, actually? Why do we have them? Why are they important for composing? And how can we apply the music theory of scales in our digital audio workstation?

Let's start by explaining what scales are. All sounds are made up of vibrating molecules in the air. They vibrate in pattern clusters we interpret as wavelengths. Frequency is the term we use to describe the number of wavelengths that pass through the air per second. The following figure shows an example of how we interpret vibrating air molecules as sound waves.

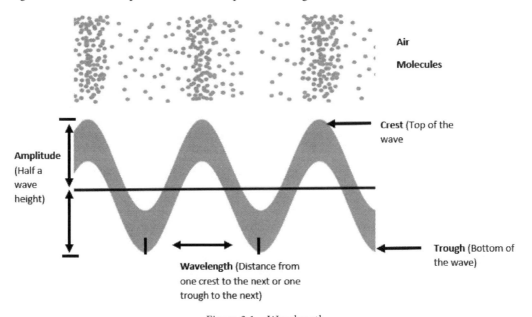

Figure 3.1 – Wavelength

Musical instruments cause air molecules to vibrate at specific frequencies. When air vibrates at a specific constant frequency, our ears interpret the noise as a note pitch. If you have a string instrument, you will be familiar with the idea of tuning your instrument strings to certain frequencies so that when you pluck a string, you get the desired pitch.

We give this a name depending on the audio frequency hit and call it a note pitch. For example, we give the frequency 220 Hz the name *A*, or more specifically *A3*, when played on a piano. A chord is defined as three or more notes played together. When you play three or more different audio wavelengths at the same time, you're creating chords.

What happens if we double the frequency of a note? The following figure shows a comparison of a wave form frequency of 220 Hz and 440 Hz.

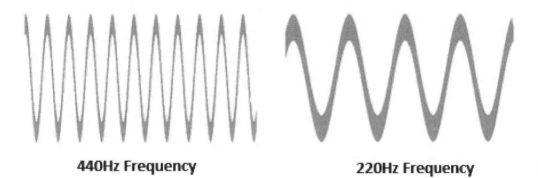

440Hz Frequency   **220Hz Frequency**

Figure 3.2 – Frequencies

The 440 Hz frequency sounds exactly twice as high as the 220 Hz frequency. We give this interval a name: an **octave**. An octave is an interval between one musical pitch and another with double the frequency. The two sounds played together sound good. This is true for any two sound frequencies where one is double the frequency of the other. All we've said so far is that a root note pairs nicely with a note an octave apart.

Okay, so the frequency 220 Hz is a note we know as *A3* and 440 Hz we know as *A4*. What about that range between 220 Hz and 440 Hz? Inside that interval, there is a range of frequencies to choose from. If we match the note 220 Hz with a note somewhere in the range of 220Hz and 440Hz, how do we know whether the combination of notes will sound good together?

Over time, we've noticed certain combinations of frequency ratios sound really good together. For example, if we use a note *A3* (frequency of 220 Hz) with a note that's an interval ratio of 3:2 (330 Hz), they will sound good together. That second note of 330 Hz is a note commonly known as *E3*. Trying to think in terms of interval ratios is confusing, though. Instead of trying to remember the names of interval ratios, we use some common terminology. In the case of a 3:2 interval ratio (*A3* paired with *E3*), we use the term **perfect fifth**.

The following table shows sound intervals that sound pleasant when accompanying a root note. The table is ranked from consonant to dissonant, **consonant** meaning the sound is in harmony with the root note and **dissonant** meaning the note doesn't harmonize well with the root note:

Interval Name	Frequency Ratio Relationship between the Notes
Root	1:1
Octave	2:1
Perfect fifth	3:2
Perfect fourth	4:3
Major third	5:4
Minor sixth	5:3
Minor third	6:5
Major sixth	8:5
Major second	9:8
Minor seventh	9:5
Minor second	16:15
Major seventh	15:8

Figure 3.3 – Consonant to dissonant

Take the perfect fifth as an example; the ratio relationship is 3:2. Our ears like the harmony of a root paired up with a sound that has a 3:2 frequency ratio. Our ears like hearing nice, evenly spaced intervals, such as 2:1, 3:2, 4:2, 5:4, and 5:3. As we venture away from these round intervals, our ears interpret the sound as more dissonant.

The most harmonious intervals are the perfect fifth, perfect fourth, major third, and minor third. If you're looking to pair notes with a root note, you'll often want to consider including these intervals.

An octave means you're comparing a root note with a note exactly double its frequency. Western music divides up an octave of music into 12 note intervals. Western music has 12 notes: *A, A#, B, C, C#, D, D#, E, F, F#, G,* and *G#*.

The following table organizes notes from smallest frequency to largest frequency assuming that we start with a root note frequency of 220 Hz. It shows the ratio between root notes in relation to other notes:

Pure Intonation Ratio Relationship between the Notes	Note	Interval Name	Pure Intonation Frequency (Hz)	12-Tone Temperament Frequency (Hz)
1:1	A3	Root	220	220
16:15	A#	Minor second (m2)	234.7	233.1
9:8	B	Major second (M2)	247.5	246.9
6:5	C	Minor third (m3)	264	261.6
5:4	C#	Major third (M3)	275	277.2
4:3	D	Perfect fourth (P4)	293.3	293.7
7:5	D#	Tritone	308	311.1
3:2	E	Perfect fifth (P5)	330	329.6
5:3	F	Minor sixth (m6)	352	349.2
8:5	F#	Major sixth (M6)	366.37	370
9:5	G	Minor seventh (m7)	396	392
15:8	G#	Major seventh (M7)	412.5	415.3
2:1	A4	Octave	440	440

Figure 3.4 – Note intervals

The preceding figure takes the range between 440 Hz and 220 Hz and divides it into 12 interval segments. You can see the note that the frequency is associated with. You may be wondering what the column is about with the title **12-Tone Equal Temperament Frequency (Hz)**.

What is 12-tone equal temperament frequency (Hz)?

In the **12-Tone Equal Temperament Frequency (Hz)** column, you'll notice that some frequencies don't line up perfectly with the ratio. For example, for a root note with a frequency of 220 Hz, a perfect fifth should be 330 Hz. However, in the **12-Tone Equal Temperament Frequency (Hz)** column, it says the frequency is 329.6 Hz. In reality, we don't tune our instrument pitch to 330 Hz; we actually tune our instruments to 329.6 Hz. Why would that be?

The reason we tune our instruments differently is so we can easily change keys on our instruments without retuning to a new key. For example, if we were to start with a root note of *D#* (308 Hz) and pair it with a note that has a frequency ratio of 3:2, that would mean we would need to pair it with an *A#* note that has a frequency of 462 Hz. But since our instrument is tuned to the key of *A*, the *A#* note is 469.3 Hz. This means that our instrument would sound out of tune. So, what do we do to fix this? We tune some notes slightly off intentionally. It's slightly off, but not really noticeably off. Tuning this way gives us the freedom to easily switch the key to our root note and have other notes in the scale sound approximately in tune.

Why does Western music use 12 notes?

Instruments like the violin and trombone allow you to hit notes that are different than 12 notes. You can play frequencies in between the 12 notes. Why are 12 note pitches commonly used? Why not more or less? What about the frequency of 226 Hz or 227 Hz? What about other interval ratios? How come they aren't appearing in this list?

Some musicians in the past have experimented with creating instruments that divide up the octaves into intervals other than 12, such as dividing an octave into 19 or 24 notes. If you play a string or brass instrument, it is possible to hit notes that are other intervals.

Over the years, we realized certain frequencies interval ratios sound good to our ears. Specifically perfect fifth, perfect fourth, major third, and minor third. Using 12 notes ensures we have easy access to the harmonious frequency ratios such as perfect fifths, perfect fourths, major thirds, and minor thirds. Although we could use additional intervals than 12, we find these usually sound more dissonant and are less pleasant to our ears. So, we use 12 notes because it enables us to create sounds that harmonize well.

What are scales?

Scales are select combinations of notes in an octave that complement each other. The notes are ordered from lowest to highest frequency. In Western music, we divide up octaves into 12 note intervals. Scales use fewer notes than 12. They are a selection of notes from the 12 that complement each other. Scales are frameworks that try to force you to play notes that sound good together.

Why are scales important for composing and how do you use scales to compose?

The mood of your music is largely set by the scale you choose. For example, if you only use notes that belong to a minor scale, your music is going to take on a sad or dark tone. If you only use notes that belong to a major scale, your music is going to sound happy and light.

By understanding the mood and tone that belong to each scale, you can choose a scale that matches your desired mood appropriately. In order to do that, we need to know what scales are available to us.

FL Studio offers support for finding what notes are included in a given scale. Let's explore tools to help us compose using scales:

1. Load up a melodic instrument such as FL Keys into the Channel rack. If you need a refresher on how to use the Channel rack or Piano roll, we discussed it in *Chapter 2, Navigating Through the Key Features of FL Studio.*

2. Open the Piano roll with your instrument and select the stamp tool.

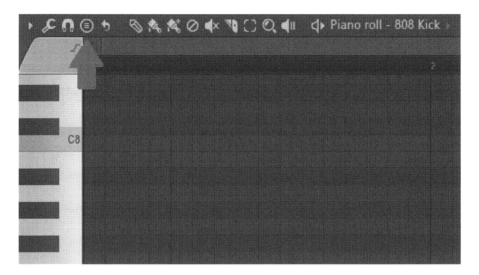

Figure 3.5 – Stamp tool

A drop-down menu will appear listing a large selection of MIDI note presets. It shows chords, scales, and suggestions for percussive sequences. Of interest to this chapter is the **Melodic Scales** selection.

3. Left-click on a scale such as the **Minor Harmonic** scale, as shown in the following screenshot:

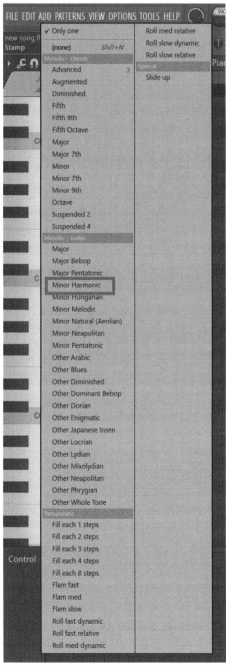

Figure 3.6 – Choose scale

This selects a series of MIDI notes (note pitches) that belong to the minor harmonic scale.

4. Left-click anywhere in the grid of the Piano roll to place the notes. After placing the scale notes, you will see something like the following screenshot.

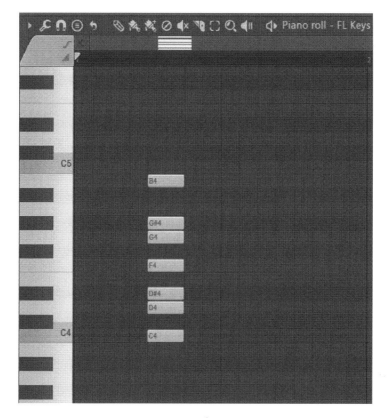

Figure 3.7 – Place notes

The notes you see belong to the minor harmonic scale. In the preceding figure, we happened to start with a tonic note of C. **Tonic note** means the first note of a scale. The notes that belong to the minor harmonic scale with a tonic note of C are C, D, D#, F, G, G#, and B. As long as I only use these included notes, I will be using notes that fit in the minor harmonic scale. Music in a harmonic minor scale tends to sound sad, beautiful, or dark, so by choosing notes in this scale, I can make my music sound sad, beautiful, or dark.

5. Using the Piano roll makes changing keys super easy. Left-click on any of the notes in the Piano roll you added. You'll notice they all get selected as a group. Shift all the notes one pitch higher as shown in the following screenshot:

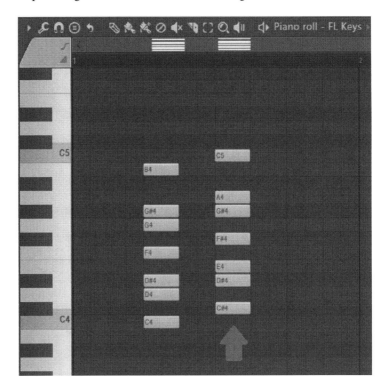

Figure 3.8 – Transpose key

By dragging all the notes up one pitch, we have transposed the notes to a new key. In this case, our notes now have a tonic note of C#. This means we are now using the minor harmonic scale of C# minor instead of C minor. The notes in this C# minor harmonic scale are C#, D#, E, F#, G#, A, and C.

Wow, transposing music to a new key was easy. We didn't have to do any calculations to transpose the notes. All we did was select the notes and move them up or down one an increment and FL Studio did all the work of transposing. If you ever had the task of trying to figure out how to transpose music, you'll realize this is a game changer. Changing musical keys in a Piano roll is incredibly easy, with almost no effort being required in trying to figure out what notes to use.

You have learned what scales are and how to change keys. But you don't yet know how to use them to get the desired tonal moods. For that, we need to introduce the concept of modes.

Understanding modes

Modes are scales, but a specific type of scale. They have some useful applications when composing music and we can use them to create specific moods.

Let's take a look at some more of the scales in the stamp tool of the Piano roll we saw in the preceding section. If you open the stamp tool again, you'll notice there are a series of scale names. Some of these scales may feel unfamiliar to you if you haven't studied music theory before. For example, you can see the scales **Aeolian**, **Pentatonic**, **Dorian**, **Locrian**, **Lydian**, **Mixolydian**, and **Phrygian**, as shown in the following screenshot, as well as many others:

Figure 3.9 – Modes

What are these? These are modes. Modes are a type of scale. The seven modes in their logical order are **Ionian**, **Dorian**, **Phrygian**, **Lydian**, **Mixolydian**, **Aeolian**, and **Locrian**. They are related to each other. To explain how, we need a visual.

Use the stamp tool to select **Major Scale** and place this on a *C* note.

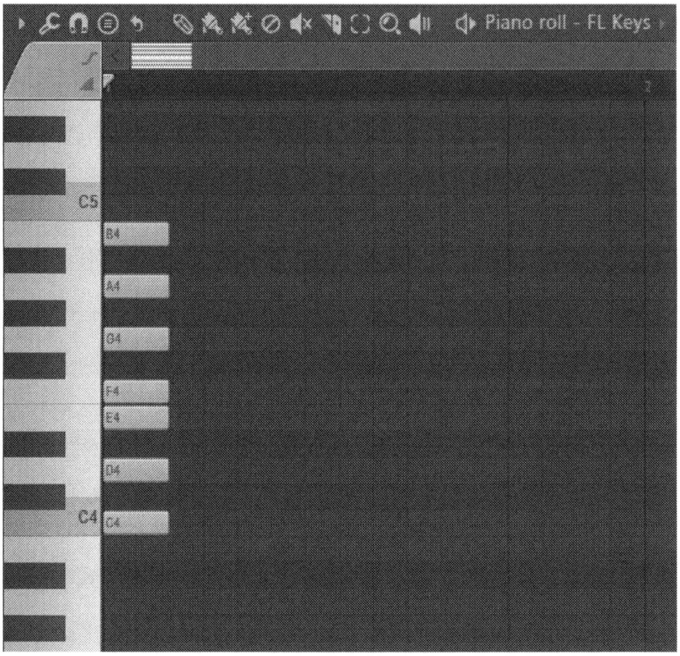

Figure 3.10 – Major Scale, also known as Ionian mode

The scale in the previous screenshot is commonly known as a **C major scale**. It's also called the **Ionian mode for C**. The term *major scale* is just a more common name for the Ionian mode. The Ionian mode is a combination of notes made up of the following:

- Root
- Major second
- Major third
- Perfect fourth
- Perfect fifth
- Major sixth
- Major seventh

When we play notes in the Ionian scale, it's generally recognized as a happy melody. Let me say this again. *Major scale = Ionian mode*. They are the same thing.

What happens if we use the same notes, but start using the second note in the Ionian mode? In other words, we take the tonic note of the Ionian scale and make it the seventh note as shown in the following screenshot.

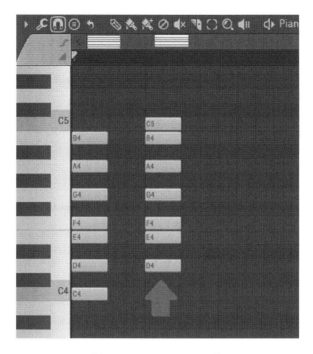

Figure 3.11 – Dorian mode

This new scale uses the same notes but starts with a tonic note of *D*. This is called the **Dorian mode**.

What just happened here? We did something quite incredible, but you might not realize the implications yet. Even though we are using the same notes as the Ionian mode, we made a new mode. This sounds like it's not a big deal until you realize that music played in the Ionian mode sounds quite different to music shifted to be played in the Dorian mode. Notes played in the Dorian mode have a distinct personality that sounds different than in the Ionian mode.

In the Ionian scale, there are seven possible different notes in the scale to choose from. Correspondingly, there are seven possible modes. As we just saw, if we shift up one note from Ionian, we end up with Dorian. If we keep shifting up, we'll end up with Phrygian, Lydian, Mixolydian, Aeolian, and finally Locrian. If we shift up one more, we'll have gone up an octave and are back to the Ionian mode again.

This is a big deal, and you'll start to realize how big a deal it is when you start composing melodies. The tonic note you start with will result in different moods for your song. Start on a tonic note of an Ionian mode and your music will sound happy and light. Start with a tonic note of an Aeolian mode and your music will sound sad, beautiful, and dark.

How to use modes

Music has a different mood depending on what mode is used. If you are composing for soundtracks, you can choose a mood and then figure out the mode that will best reflect it.

The following list details modes and the moods associated with them, along with some real-life examples. I encourage you to quickly google the songs so you have an idea of what music can be created using different modes:

- **Ionian mode**: Major key, happy music.

  Let It Be – The Beatles

  Free Fallin – Tom Petty

- **Dorian mode**: Jazzy. It's a minor scale with a raised sixth.

  PokemonGo Theme Song

  Ballad of the Goddess – Hajime Wakai & Takeshi Hama (The Legend of Zelda: Skyward Sword)

  Halo – Martin O'Donnell and Michael Salvatori

- **Phrygian mode**: Dark, emotional.

  Time in a Bottle – Jim Croce

  Dr Who theme song – Murray Gold

- **Lydian mode**: Jazzy, worldly, triumphant sounds. It's a major scale with a raised fourth.

  Six Feet Under theme – Thomas Newman

  Superman Theme song – John Williams

  E.T. theme song – John Williams

- **Mixolydian mode**: Great for triumphant sounds with brass and strings. It's a major scale with a lowered seventh.

  Staff Roll – Super Mario Galaxy

  Bundle of Joy – Michael Giacchino (Inside Out Film)

- **Aeolian mode**: Minor key, sad, beautiful, melancholic, dark.

  Manners Maketh Man – Henry Jackman and Matthew Margeson (Kingsman: The Secret Service)

  The Medallion Calls – Klaus Badelt, Hans Zimmer (Pirates of the Caribbean)

  The Game Is On – David Arnold and Michael Price (Sherlock)

- **Locrian mode**: A bit strange sounding. Not used very often unless you want odd-sounding music. Mostly used for jazz.

If you're trying to achieve a mood and tone for your music, consider choosing a mode that fits your mood/tone and compose notes that fit within it.

What notes are in my scale?

How do I know what notes to use for a scale? The nice thing with FL Studio is that you don't have to worry about what notes are in any given scale. The Piano roll stamp tool helps you instantly find the notes to be used.

In the stamp tool, you'll notice that there are a lot more scales than the ones we have covered so far in this chapter. Each of these scales provides its own unique mood. For example, using a blues scale makes your music sound like blues genre music. I encourage you to experiment with picking different scales and see how they change the mood and tone of your compositions.

If you need to check what notes are in a given scale, a great website with visual references is www.pianoscales.org. This website lists lots of available scales.

In order to find the section on modes, navigate to the **Jazz Scale Piano** tab as shown in the following screenshot:

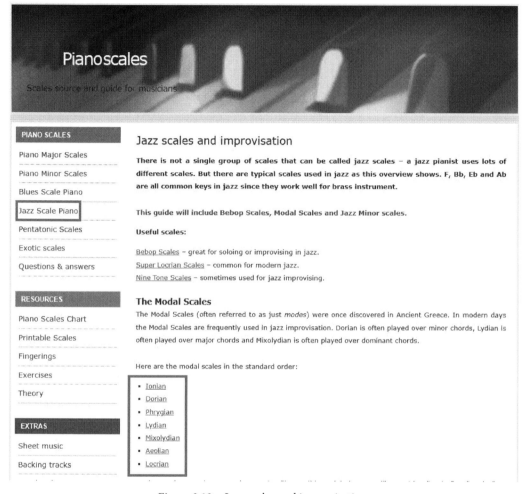

Figure 3.12 – Jazz scales and improvisation

Once on the **Jazz Scale Piano** page, you'll see a list of the modal scales. If you select one of them, you will see notes used for the mode starting with a chosen tonic note.

You'll then see a list of piano diagrams illustrating what notes are allowed to be used for the mode, as shown in the following screenshot.

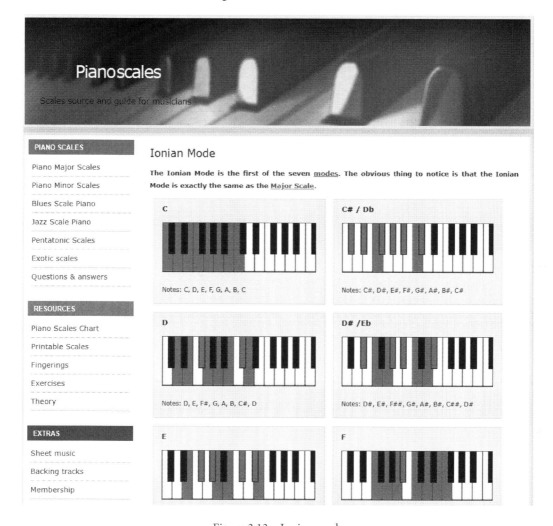

Figure 3.13 – Ionian mode

Using the website, it's easy to identify what notes can be used for playing a song in any scale.

We've learned about scales and modes. But is there a reference to visually see what scale to use when composing? Yes, there is: it's called using ghost notes (muted notes).

Using ghost notes for scale reference

Here's a little trick that's helpful when composing within a scale. It's called using ghost notes (aka muted notes). Ghost notes can be used to visually identify what notes are in your chosen scale:

1. Add a melodic instrument to the Channel rack. For example, choose **FL Keys**.

2. Name the instrument in the Channel rack, such as `Ghost Notes`.

3. Create a duplicate of the instrument in the Channel rack and give it a different name, such as `Piano`.

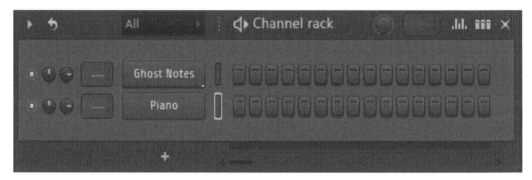

Figure 3.14 – Created instrument called Ghost Notes

4. Open up the Piano roll for the instrument called **Ghost Notes**.

5. Open up the stamp tool and select a desired scale and add it to the Piano roll. For example, you can select the major scale.

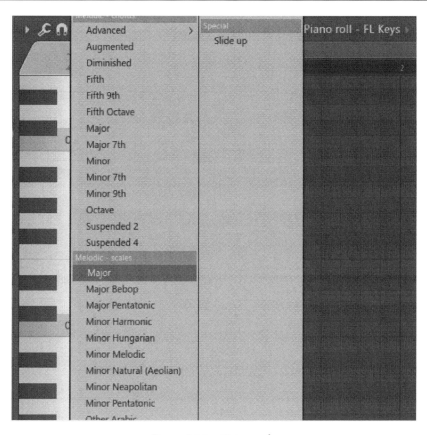

Figure 3.15 – Major scale

6. Mute the notes in the scale you added. You can use the mute tool at the top of the Piano roll and then drag over the notes you want to mute. Another method is to double right-click next to the notes you want to mute and hold and drag over the notes you want to mute.

The following screenshot shows the muted notes in the scale.

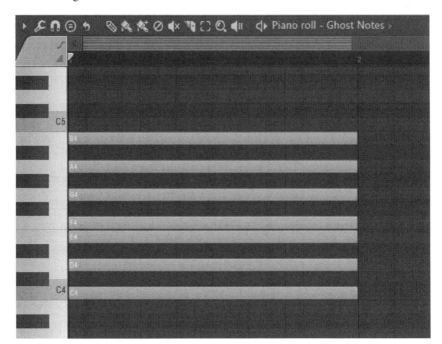

Figure 3.16 – Muted notes for reference

When the pattern is played, the instrument will be silent. However, the notes act as a visual reference to help us when composing. They provide us with a visual to guide what notes are allowed to be used.

7. Switch instruments in the Piano roll, such as to the one we named `Piano`.

8. In the Piano roll grid, you'll see a faint outline of the muted notes played by the **Ghost Notes** instrument. These are notes in the scale that can be used.

The following screenshot shows that although we are composing notes for the **Piano** instrument, we can see the notes used in the **Ghost Notes** instrument.

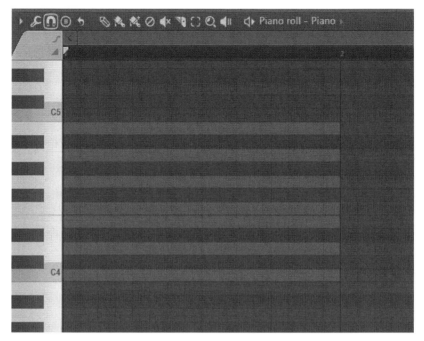

Figure 3.17 – Muted notes in scale

In the preceding screenshot, we have the **Piano** instrument open in the Piano roll. The faded notes are the muted notes from the **Ghost Notes** instrument.

9.   Any of the notes you see in the **Ghost Notes** instrument are acceptable choices that fit into the C major scale. You can now add notes with ease as you know all the notes that can be used.

The following screenshot shows an example of adding notes that overlap the ghost notes.

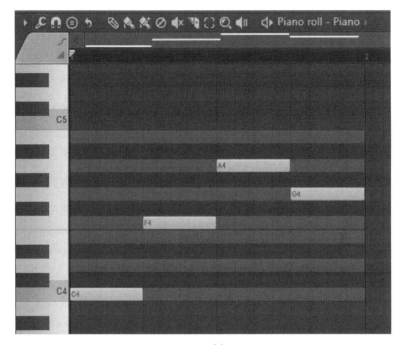

Figure 3.18 – Adding notes

This technique can be used for any scale and can save you a lot of time. You no longer have to spend effort figuring out what notes are in a given scale. You can just use the stamp tool to plunk down scale notes and instantly start composing over them.

We have learned how to compose with scales; next, let's learn how music terminology helps us use scales.

Understanding sharps and flats

Later in this chapter, we'll explain how to use the music chord wheel tool for composing. But the chord wheel requires that you first understand what sharps and flats are. On a piano, you'll notice there are white notes and black notes. The white notes are whole tones. We assign whole tones the letter names *C*, *D*, *E*, *F*, *G*, *A*, and *B*. The black notes on a piano are semitones between the white notes. We call these **sharps** and **flats**. Sharp are indicated by a # symbol. Flats are indicated by a ♭ symbol. The following diagram shows piano notes with note labels.

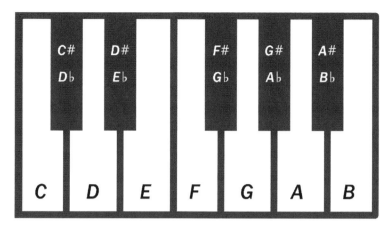

Figure 3.19 – Sharps and flats

You'll notice the black notes each have two names on them. For example, the black note between the *C* and *D* note has the name *C#* and *D*♭. *C#* and *D*♭ mean the same note.

To clarify, sharps and flats don't mean black notes. Sharp just means a raised note by a semitone and a flat just means to lower a note by a semitone. This allows you notation freedom, such as if you wanted to do something with double sharps and double flats.

Why do we have two different terms of sharps and flats for the same note? The reason is to help clarify information for the reader.

Here's an example of how music notation would be confusing if we didn't have rules for when to use sharps and flats. If we were to have a *C* chord: *C*, *E*, and *G*, and I wanted the minor version of that *C* chord, what would I call the notes? The correct way is to call them *C*, *E*♭, and *G*. This way, we can maintain the same note names as the major key. If we were to use the sharp naming for this chord, it would be *C*, *D#*, and *G*. Either way you name it, we're lowering by a semitone, but one way maintains the letter naming. Maintaining the lettering makes it easier for musicians trying to read the music.

Sharps or flats are listed at the beginning of sheet music to tell a musician what key a song should be played in. It's listed in what's called a **key signature**. The following screenshot shows an example of a key signature:

Figure 3.20 – Key signature

https://upload.wikimedia.org/wikipedia/commons/1/1d/Db_minor_key_signature.png

A key signature shows the symbols treble clef and bass clef and then lists the number of sharps or flats to the right. This tells the musician what sharps and flats are to be used for the piece. The musician can then use this information to figure out what key the song should be played in.

We know what sharps and flats are and key signatures. With this information, we can now learn how to use **the Circle of Fifths chord wheel**.

Using the Circle of Fifths chord wheel

The **Circle of Fifths chord wheel** is a visual tool used by musicians as a cheat sheet for music theory. It's a diagram containing a list of key signatures and it conveys a large amount of information very quickly to the reader.

The Circle of Fifths diagram can be used for a variety of purposes. It can be used as a reference for transposing music from one key to another. Live musicians may use it to assist with improvising when trying to figure out what key to use. As a composer, you'll likely want to use this tool whenever you want to change keys, such as changing back and forth from major to minor. The following diagram shows a simple version of the Circle of Fifths.

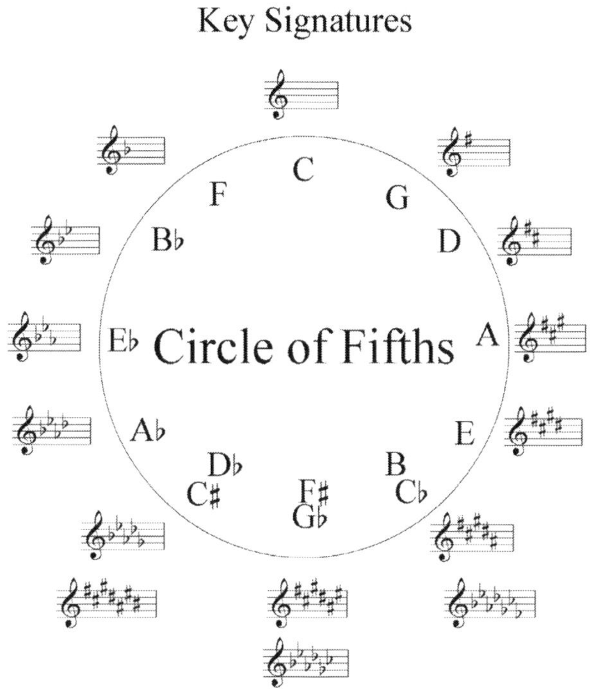

Key Signatures

Figure 3.21 – Circle of Fifths

https://commons.wikimedia.org/wiki/File:Music_Scale_Theory_-_Circle_of_Fifths.png

Starting at the top center, the inner circle lists the name of the major key (Ionian mode), in this case, C. The outside of the circle lists the music theory key signature notation for the key. It starts with the key of C, which has no sharps and flats in the scale.

Remember earlier in this chapter we learned that a perfect fifth is a nice and neat way of saying we moved from a root note to a second note with a frequency interval relationship of 3:2 – for example, moving from the note C to G. This results in a combination of notes that sound very good when played together. If we were to move a perfect fifth from the root note C, we would land upon the note G. The key G has a single sharp in the scale. If we were to move up a perfect fifth from the root note G, we would land on the note D. The key of D has two sharps in the scale.

Trying to recall this from memory is tedious. You're likely already getting confused trying to keep track of all these letters unless you have a piano in front of you to look at. The Circle of Fifths will make it so that you won't have to memorize any of the information.

The Circle of Fifths makes it easy to figure out what notes are in each scale. On the diagram, you move a perfect fifth each time you increment clockwise around the Circle of Fifths. For example, start at the key of C at the top center. If you move one increment to the right, you'll land on the key of G, which is exactly a perfect fifth.

As you continue moving clockwise around the circle, the number of sharps increases by one each time until you reach the key of C# major.

If you start with the key of C and move anticlockwise around the circle, you'll be moving down a perfect fifth. Moving key signatures anticlockwise increments in flats until you reach the key of C♭ major.

In other words, this diagram shows how all the major scale keys related to one another. It shows the difference in sharps and flats between scales.

So, the Circle of Fifths can help us identify what notes are in a major key. Is that all this diagram does? Oh no…it does much more. We're just getting started. Let's take a look at a slightly more detailed diagram of the Circle of Fifths.

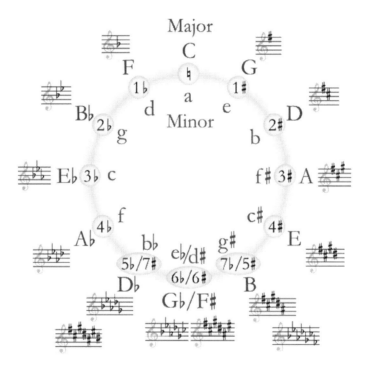

Figure 3.22 – Detailed Circle of Fifths
https://upload.wikimedia.org/wikipedia/commons/4/40/Circle_of_fifths_deluxe_pale_beads.png

In the innermost circle, it lists the relative minors of the Circle of Fifths. These are the minor scales that use the same notes as the major keys. They have the same key signature.

Whoa…there are multiple scales that use the same notes and it all lines up this neatly? Is this a coincidence? No, it's not. In fact, it must be exactly this way. Let's explain why.

Remember earlier in this chapter we learned about modes. All modes use the same notes for a given a scale; they just use a different tonic note. The first mode we call Ionian and it means the same thing as the major scale. The fifth mode we call Aeolian and it is the same thing as the natural minor scale. The natural minor uses the same notes as the major scale but starts with a different tonic note.

In theory, you could list out all the modes using a Circle of Fifths diagram if you could be bothered, but it would be overly detailed to look at. Instead, in most cases the Circle of Fifths diagram lists just the major and/or minor keys for each key signature.

Okay, there are a lot of super cool features in this diagram, but how do I use this in practice? When you're composing, there are times when you want to change the key of a song. This Circle of Fifths diagram can help you change keys.

Why would you want to change the key of a song? Let's take a huge step back and look at how we interpret changes in sound.

If you want your music to feel like it's increasing in energy, there are several ways to do so. You could increase the velocity or articulation intensity (discussed in *Chapter 4, Orchestral MIDI Composing*), increase the speed, or in the case of the topic of this chapter, increase the pitch of the sound itself.

By changing keys and transposing notes to another key, you can increase or decrease note pitches and make it sound like the music energy level is increasing or decreasing. If you want to make it sound like your music is changing in energy, one way to do this is to move to a new key. Also, changing keys adds variation, which can be useful. It allows you to essentially play the same melody twice while not sounding repetitive to the listener.

Let's get back to the Circle of Fifths. If we want to change keys, how do we use the Circle of Fifths to do so? By moving clockwise to the next key on the Circle of Fifths, you increase the number of sharps in the key, but only by one. If we were to start with the key of C, which has no sharps, and move one increment to the right on the Circle of Fifths, we would end up in the key of G, which has one sharp. This means that the scale itself has only slightly changed. It's a slight transition to the listener.

On the other hand, if you were to start with the major key of C and transition to the key of F# major, it would sound like an extreme change to the listener. We'd be adding six sharps. What does this mean? It means that if you want to change keys, it sounds less jarring to the listener if you move clockwise or anticlockwise around the Circle of Fifths by small increments at a time. Large movements around the Circle of Fifths sound like extreme jumps to the listener.

If you were to start with the key of *C* major and wanted to change keys using the Circle of Fifths, a good choice would be to move one increment clockwise to *G* major, or one increment anticlockwise to *F* major. Either of these changes in keys would be a subtle transition to a listener. The more key increments you jump at once, the more jarring the transition will be.

The Circle of Fifths chord wheel has multiple benefits. It allows you to quickly identify what key signature belongs to each scale so you know what notes can be played. It also allows you to identify what scales can be smoothly transitioned into when changing keys.

Summary

In this chapter, we learned about a series of tools and frameworks that can be used when creating music. We learned about motifs, leitmotifs, and themes and how to use them to come up with ideas for what to compose.

We learned about scales, what they are, how they help us figure out what notes to use, and how to apply them in practice. We learned about modes and how they're used. We learned how to use the FL Studio Piano roll stamp tool to easily add notes for any given scale without having to learn and memorize the scale details. Finally, we learned how to use the Circle of Fifths chord wheel tool to see how scales relate to each other and how to smoothly transition between scales.

In the next chapter, we'll learn techniques for composing orchestral compositions.

4

Orchestral MIDI Composing

In this chapter, you will learn about the tools you can use to create orchestral music. Specifically, you will learn how to make orchestral music using MIDI programming. We'll get you set up with tools you can use to compose such music. Along the way, you'll learn about techniques for string arrangements, chord progressions, how to make your programmed instruments sound realistic, and some mixing best practices.

In this chapter, we're going to cover the following topics:

- Why learn orchestral composing?
- Recommended orchestral tool plugins
- Using velocity, articulations, and expression
- Orchestral MIDI programming
- Tips for composing orchestral chord progressions
- Considerations for mixing orchestral compositions

Why learn orchestral composing?

When composing for films, you must be able to compose for a wide range of styles and genres. Although you may have a specific preference in a niche genre, having the ability to switch from one style to another gives you more opportunities. Having the ability to compose orchestral compositions gives you an overall well-rounded skill set of techniques and tools to draw upon.

Becoming good at composing music means you have a versatile composing skill set. Composing orchestral music is a great way to get exposure to a wide range of composing situations. Composing orchestral MIDI music forces you to have experience with the following elements:

- Understanding how to compose chord progressions and spread the instrumentation among different instruments

- Understanding the limits and opportunities that live acoustic instruments present

- Understanding how to make instrument plugins sound more real and less synthetic

- Using percussion to generate movement and knowing how to transition between instrument sections

- Arranging instrumentation. Balancing volumes and using equalization to give frequency space to instrument sections

These skills are acquired as a byproduct of having experience in composing orchestral music. This chapter will provide you with the foundation to get started. We'll start with the tools that you need to compose and then we'll get to the interesting stuff and learn about orchestral MIDI composing so that you can compose music yourself.

Before we can begin though, we need some orchestral instruments.

Recommended orchestral tool plugins

To create orchestral music, you need orchestral instrument plugins. If you're new to this, I recommend that you play around with FLEX first. It's an instrument plugin that's free and comes with all versions of FL Studio.

You can load up FLEX by inserting FLEX into the Channel rack, as shown in the following screenshot:

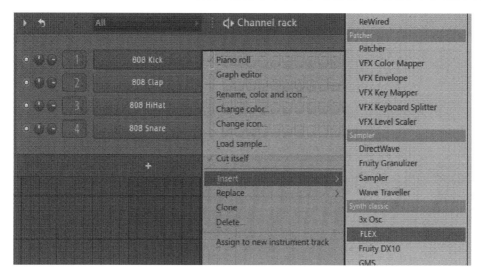

Figure 4.1 – Inserting FLEX

This will load up the FLEX plugin. At the top left of FLEX, you'll see a tab called **FREE**. Navigate to it. This will show a list of free plugins you can download to FLEX. Download them. Once you've done that, FLEX will be populated with plugin packs such as **Essential Strings**, as shown in the following screenshot:

Figure 4.2 – FLEX

When you install the free FLEX preset packs that come with FLEX, you'll find an instrument library to work with that contains orchestral instruments. For example, FLEX includes preset packs for **Essential Bass Guitars**, **Essential Guitars**, **Essential Pianos**, **Essential Strings**, and **Essential Winds**.

In the **Essential Strings** and **Essential Winds** packs, you'll find different articulations for the instruments. In the pack entitled **General Midi Library**, you'll find drumkits. These can provide a great percussion library for your compositions, as shown in the following screenshot:

Figure 4.3 – FLEX drumkits

General Midi Library also lists a range of instrument presets for orchestral instruments such as harps, saxophones, church choirs, timpanis, vibraphones, tom-toms, glockenspiels, guitars, acoustic bass instruments, woodblocks, and xylophones. If you're looking for some less commonly used instruments, you'll also find banjos, bagpipes, and church organs.

FLEX allows you to search for instrument sounds by name or by the instrument tags associated with the sound. The following screenshot shows the tags for instrument types and styles you can search by:

Figure 4.4 – FLEX tags

By selecting tags by type or style, you can filter out instruments in FLEX to find sounds that are exactly what you are looking for. There's also a search bar at the bottom where you can search for instruments by name.

FLEX is one of the most intuitive instrument plugins I've come across and, as I mentioned previously, it's included free with FL Studio.

Recommended paid instrument plugins

FLEX is fine for newbies, but it's lacking compared to some of the best orchestral plugins on the market. When you want to spend some money and get some state-of-the-art instrument plugins, here are some of my recommendations:

- **Native Instruments** (`https://www.native-instruments.com/`) offers a huge selection of instrument plugins and effects. Native Instrument products are an industry staple among music producers and composers around the world. They also sell MIDI keyboards, which are commonly used by professionals. I'm a big fan of their products.

- **EastWest Sounds** (`https://www.soundsonline.com/`) offers state-of-the-art orchestral instruments for film scoring that have been used in many Hollywood films throughout the years.

Their plugin, **Opus**, which came out in 2021, is a game-changer. It's an orchestral library plugin with all the instruments you'd expect to find in an orchestra. But what sets Opus apart is a feature called **Orchestrator**. This feature provides a set of MIDI presets that are intended for orchestral compositions. It can provide suggestions for orchestral compositions, which can then be tweaked to your liking.

If you're trying to make the sound of a traditional orchestra, Orchestrator is your one-stop shop. It's a fantastic tool for learning how MIDI instruments and articulations can be used masterfully in an orchestra.

- **Spectrasonic's Omnisphere plugin** (`https://www.spectrasonics.net/products/omnisphere/`) offers a huge selection of instruments that are great for film scoring.

With that, we've learned about some of the tools we can use to compose orchestral music. Having instrument plugins is only the first step, though. Now, we need to learn how to use them. So, how can we use them effectively?

What makes instrument plugins sound real?

Beginner musicians sound significantly different than professionals, even when they play the same song with the same notes. Why might this be?

Let's use a piano as an example. A piano makes a sound when a key is pressed. This causes a hammer to hit a string, which makes a sound. When a beginner plays a song, they don't have much control over the instrument. The notes likely have the same volume, their pacing may be all over the place, and the player isn't intentionally adding their personality to the performance.

When a professional plays, they have full control over the instrument. The player carefully manipulates the speed at which the instrument is played. They decide how loud to play each note. Each hand may play at different volumes than the other hand throughout the piece. Their right hand, which usually plays the main melody, will likely play slightly louder than their left hand, which will be playing the accompaniment.

The speed may increase or decrease throughout the piece to add a sense of momentum. The volume will vary, such as lowering in the calmer verse and then rising when the chorus hits. The performer will be keenly listening and reacting to the song throughout. They know that for music to feel more impactful when loud, it helps to proceed with softer music. Whenever you want to emphasize movement or sound, it helps to contrast it with something.

To make your music sound interesting to the listener, you need to introduce variation. There are many ways to add variation. For example, you can vary the melody, instruments, volumes, effects, and fade these changes in and out as you go. These are effective and will be discussed throughout this chapter.

Now, let's discuss how to use software to mimic instrument-playing techniques that are used by live musicians. This will help to make your sounds appear more realistic and enjoyable to listen to. The three techniques we will learn about are velocity, articulations, and expression. All three are very easy to learn and you'll be able to pick up and apply these techniques right away in your compositions.

Using velocity

Velocity is how rapidly and forcefully a key on a keyboard is pressed when a player initially hits a key. Velocity simulates the behavior of a piano mechanism. A note that's struck on a piano is louder if the key is struck more forcefully.

Velocity is related to, but not the same as, volume. Increasing the velocity does increase note volume, but it also increases the intensity with which the note is played. Increasing velocity makes it appear that more emphasis and energy has been put into the note.

Velocity is usually referred to when discussing pianos. However, almost all percussive-like instruments (in plugin form) can control note velocity. For example, you can usually control velocity on pianos, harps, xylophones, vibraphones, drums, cymbals, and chimes. Essentially, any instrument that involves hitting it likely has a velocity control.

Let's look at an example of how to use velocity effectively:

1. Load up **FL Keys** or another piano instrument in the **Channel rack**.

2. Open the instrument in the Piano roll.

3. Left-click the Piano roll to add some notes:

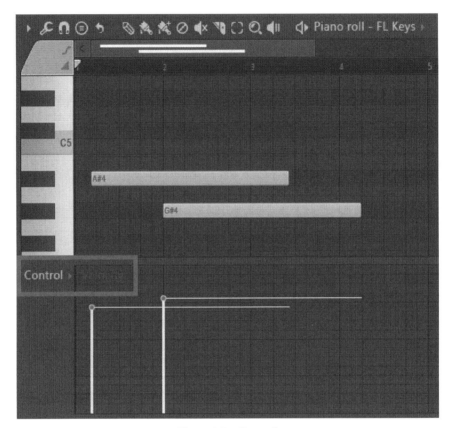

Figure 4.5 – Control

After adding these notes, you should see something similar to the preceding screenshot. At the bottom left of the Piano roll, you'll see **Control**, followed by the current control that's been enabled. By default, **Velocity** is enabled.

4. If you don't see **Velocity**, left-click on **Control**. A drop-down menu will appear, where you can select **Note velocity**:

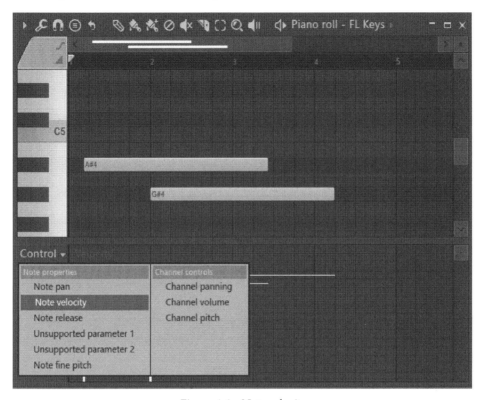

Figure 4.6 – Note velocity

Once you've selected **Note velocity**, the bottom grid will become a control for note velocity. For each note that is added, a line will appear in the bottom grid of the Piano roll, indicating the note velocity. By left-clicking the bottom grid while a note is selected, you can change the height of the line. The longer the height, the greater the velocity.

5. Left-click to add differing velocity for your notes. The following screenshot shows an example of this:

Figure 4.7 – Changing note velocity

In the preceding screenshot, you can see that I've added increasing velocity for my notes. As the notes play, they will become louder and more punctuated.

6. Once you have selected a note, you can fine-tune the velocity by holding down the left *Alt* key and then scrolling with your mouse wheel.

Great – we know how to control velocity! So what? Why do we care? Controlling velocity allows our instruments to mimic how live musicians play. Strategically choosing note velocity makes our instrument plugins sound lifelike.

To add realism to your sounds, you'll want to take each melody you compose and break its velocity down in the following steps:

1. Identify the most important melody and assign it a higher overall velocity than the accompanying melodies.

2. For each melody and accompaniment, identify the overall momentum of the melody. Assign velocities to emphasize the movement.

This may sound confusing, so let's break it down.

When a pianist plays, they play multiple melodies at once. Usually, they play at least two, but there could be more. Their left hand is playing one melody (usually the bassline chord progression), while their right hand is playing a second melody (usually the main melody). These melodies play off each other and provide a contrast.

In a simple scenario, the pianist's right hand plays the main melody. This involves playing the notes higher up on the keyboard (higher in pitch). At the same time, their left hand plays the accompaniment lower on the keyboard (lower in pitch).

The following screenshot shows an example where the main melody, which is being played by the pianist's right hand, has a higher velocity than the accompaniment notes that are being played with their left hand:

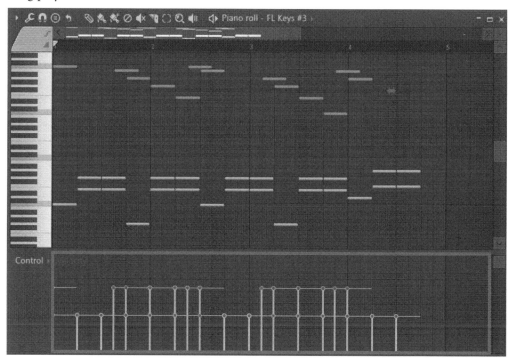

Figure 4.8 – Higher velocity played by the pianist's right hand

In the preceding screenshot, you can see two levels of velocity. I've assigned a higher velocity to the higher pitch notes and a lower velocity to the lower notes. When this melody plays, the higher-pitched melody will stand out since it has a higher velocity.

With that, we've achieved *Step 1* by isolating our main melody and the accompanying melody. Next, we must look at each melody and assign individual velocities to emphasize the melody's overall momentum.

In the following screenshot, you can see just the right-hand melody. For each note, I've assigned individual velocities. These fluctuations make the melody seem less robotic and more lifelike:

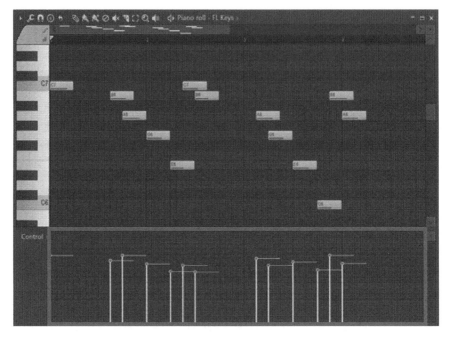

Figure 4.9 – Melody velocity of the right hand

You may be wondering whether you should increase velocity or decrease velocity for notes. What value should you choose? I can't give you that answer. What velocity you choose is subject to preference and will depend on your musical piece. Here are a few pointers, though:

- The more prominent the melody, the more dynamic range you can have. Your ears will notice the changes in dynamics. If you want your listener to be focusing on an instrument, you can change the dynamics more.

- Although velocity is often tied to volume, it's better to think of volume as a separate effect. You can adjust the volume later when you're mixing volumes and/or with compression effects. Think about velocity as how much energy and intensity you want to be inserted into playing each note. You can have a very low velocity to create soft sounds on your instruments and then hike up the volume in the mixing stage.

- If you want an instrument to take focus, increase its velocity relative to other instruments. If you want an instrument to leave focus, decrease its velocity. The same idea applies to volume too. Increasing the volume of an instrument focuses your attention on it, while decreasing it tends to make it seem less important.

With that, we've learned how to use velocity to add realism to percussive instruments, but how do we add realism to non-percussive instruments? For that, we need articulations.

Using articulations

When you're using instrument plugins that attempt to mimic live instruments, you will need to experiment with instrument articulations to add realism and interest to the sound. There are many types of articulations, and these are instrument-specific. Articulation refers to the transition between notes. For example, articulations include slurs, phrase marks, staccatos, staccatissimos, accents, sforzandos, rinforzandos, and legatos.

Here's a reference list of articulations that you may encounter:

- **Legato (slurs)**: These are long and drawn out and blend one note into the next. They often include a short half-step rise at the beginning of the sample. On string instruments, this can be done by sliding a finger along the string while moving continuously from one note to the next.

- **Staccato**: These are short and quick. It's easy to identify that one note has finished before the next. They are often thought of as the opposite of playing legato notes, and there's lots of space between notes. On string instruments, this involves the player alternating between up and down bow movements.

- **Crescendo**: This provides a continuous increase in the volume of a sound. With sampled instruments, it sounds more natural than a crossfade.

- **Decrescendo**: This provides a continuous decrease in the volume of a sound. With sampled instruments, it sounds more natural than a crossfade.

- **Glissando**: There are two possible meanings here. In general, it means a short upward run before the starting note. On harps, this means strumming the strings instead of plucking them.

- **Sustain**: This involves holding a note out until the next note, though this does not prepare the player for the following note. Usually, these samples are looped so that they can be played indefinitely. If you use sustain notes on their own, they may sound quite fake. To make them sound more realistic, you'll need to use expression automation to blend a sequence of sustained chords into the next sequence. We'll show you how to use expressions later in this chapter.

- **Trill**: This is a rapid alternating between two notes.

- **Sforzando**: This involves playing a note with extra force to add more emphasis to it over other notes near it.

- **Vibrato**: This changes the pitch of a note. In some articulations, vibrato starts after a slight delay, which allows faster sequences of notes to be performed before vibrato is applied.

The following is a list of string instrument-specific articulations:

- **Martelé**: This is where the bow pushes on each string and the sound stops between notes. This makes each note strongly accented.

- **Pizzicato**: This involves plucking the string instrument using fingers instead of a bow, which creates a short sound that cuts through the rest of the orchestra.

- **Spiccato**: This is a playing method where the bow bounces off the string while playing each note.

- **Tremelo**: This is where the same notes are repeated by quickly alternating between the bow strokes without leaving the bow. This is often used in horror films.

On some orchestral instruments, you may have the option to use key switches. This is where hitting certain MIDI notes will cause different articulations to turn on.

So far, we've learned about a list of articulations, but it's hard to imagine what this means until you've heard them. Let's look at a quick example so that you can see articulations in action:

1. Load up two or three instances of the FLEX plugin in the **Channel** rack.

2. Navigate to **Essential Strings** or **Essential Winds**. You'll find a list of different instrument articulations, as shown in the following screenshot:

Figure 4.10 – FLEX articulations

3. For each instance of FLEX, choose a different instrument articulation. For example, you may wish to pick **Violins Staccato**, **Violins Pizzicato**, or **Violins Sustain**.

    Each of these instrument articulations will provide a different sound for the instrument.

Instrument articulations are important for mimicking realism from a live player. While playing, live musicians constantly alternate the articulations they're playing. They'll jump from short staccato notes to long legato notes. They'll crescendo and decrescendo in volume and add emphasis to notes at various stages.

When you compose for the violin, for example, you'll want to include a variety of articulations in your sound to mimic a real instrument. After composing a melody, you can load up several versions of your violin instrument with different articulations (or use key switches). You can then assign melody notes to the desired instrument articulation. You must do this for each orchestral instrument. Do this strategically and you'll find that your instruments sound very lifelike and much more interesting than without articulations.

With that, we've learned about instrument articulations. Next, let's learn about expression.

Using expression

On sustain articulations, where you're using string, brass, and woodwinds, you may notice that changing the velocity doesn't seem to do anything. These instruments may or may not use velocity. Velocity is intended for instruments that involve physically hitting the instrument to produce the sound. Since nothing is being hit with certain string, brass, and woodwind articulations, how do we control the intensity of the sound?

Some instrument plugins allow you to control an effect called **expression**. If you have a MIDI keyboard with a mod wheel, often, the mod wheel is hooked up to this *expression* effect by default. Expression controls the intensity of the sound. You'll notice similarities between expression and velocity. Increasing expression, similar to increasing velocity, will increase the intensity of the sound.

By default, FL Studio doesn't come with any instruments that use expression (that I am aware of). You will need an instrument that has a dedicated expression controller. Examples of such instruments include Native Instruments orchestral instrument plugins or EastWest orchestral plugins, but there are lots of orchestral instrument plugins available on the market that have an expression effect. You can find some for free by doing a quick Google search for `orchestral instrument vst plugins`.

What is expression good for?

Automating expression is useful for a variety of situations. Expression can be used in the following scenarios:

- Increasing or decreasing the intensity of your instruments. With orchestral string, brass, or woodwind instruments, adjusting expression is generally preferable over changing volume. Changing expression sounds more natural and lifelike. With a string instrument, the tonal intensity usually increases when the player plays louder. It's not just a volume change – the whole sound changes too.

- Expression helps make the transition between the sustain chords feel more natural. Sustain note chords can sound fake and flat when you're transitioning from one chord to the next. Why? Usually, a sustain chord has a slow attack when the first note occurs. When you hit the next chord, you have to hear the slow attack again when, what you actually want is to continue from the first chord sound into the second. You can automate expression to make this transition less noticeable.

> **Note**
>
> Some instruments include legato articulations. Legato articulations sound reasonably realistic when transitioning between notes. However, the notes are usually limited to single notes at a time rather than chords. To get around this issue, if you wanted you could load up several instance of the plugin using legato articulations and have each instance hit different chord notes.

Manually adding expression to your orchestral instruments

Let's learn how to automate expression for our instruments. First, let's learn about the manual method. After that, we'll learn about the fine-tuned method, which requires you to have a MIDI keyboard with a mod wheel.

To add expression, you need an orchestra instrument that has an expression effect that can be automated. Usually, string, woodwind, and brass instrument plugins come with this effect. I recommend the Native Instruments or EastWest instrument plugins, as suggested at the beginning of this chapter, but you can use any that you like.

In the following steps, I assume that you have an orchestral plugin. If not, you will need to acquire one before you can follow the remaining steps. In my example, I am using an EastWest orchestral instrument; FL Studio does not come with this instrument by default:

1. Go to the plugin options at the top left of your orchestral instrument plugin and select the **Browse parameters** option:

Figure 4.11 – Browse parameters

After selecting **Browse parameters**, a list of all the plugin effects that are available for your instrument will appear in the Browser. Hopefully, your plugin will have an *expression* effect.

2. Right-click on the expression and choose **Create automation clip**:

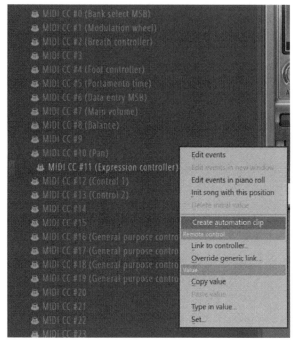

Figure 4.12 – Create automation clip

This will create an automation clip in the playlist.

3. Then, left-click in the automation curve to draw and shape the curve. Increasing the curve will increase expression; decreasing it will reduce it.

    The following screenshot shows an example of me automating an expression curve for my string sustain chords:

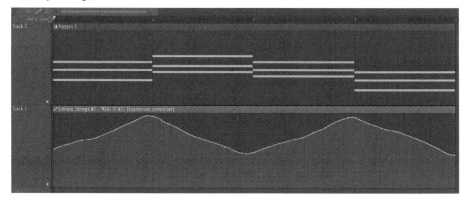

Figure 4.13 – Automating an expression in the playlist

In the preceding screenshot, we can see the playlist. In this playlist, we can see the MIDI chord pattern and expression automation curve we just created.

To make the expression effect feel more realistic, it can be a good idea to change the direction of the expression slope when you change chords.

In the preceding screenshot, I used an extreme example of automating expression. Here, we can see that the slope changes from moving up and down at the same time to changing from one MIDI chord to the next. In some situations, this may make your chord transitions sound more lifelike.

Fine-tuned method for adding expression to your orchestral instruments

If you have a MIDI keyboard with a mod wheel and your instrument connects the mod wheel to an expression effect, you can record expression automation directly while playing the song. If this is the case, it's very easy to record expression.

Let's learn how:

1. Press the record button (automation, score), as highlighted in the following screenshot. A pop-up menu will appear.

2. Select the **Notes and automation** option, as shown in the following screenshot:

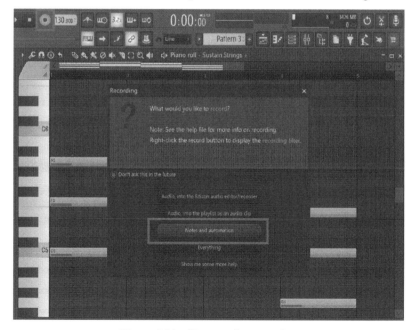

Figure 4.14 – Notes and automation

If you don't have notes already, play notes with your MIDI keyboard while recording. Alternatively, you can have the notes already inputted in the Piano roll, and just record your mod wheel automation on top of your existing notes.

While the notes are playing, move the mod wheel to control the instrument's expression. Moving the mod wheel up will increase the expression's intensity, while moving it down will decrease the expression's intensity.

The following figure shows an example of a mod wheel on a MIDI keyboard:

Figure 4.15 – Mod wheel

(https://commons.wikimedia.org/wiki/File:Moog_LP_Pitch_%26_Mod_Wheel.jpg)

If you want to use both hands while playing the MIDI keyboard instead of having one hand on a mod wheel, you could connect an expression pedal to your MIDI keyboard. Then, you can automate the expression using your foot while playing notes with both hands. The following figure shows an example of an expression pedal:

Figure 4.16 – Expression pedal

(https://commons.wikimedia.org/wiki/File:KORG_CX-3_(2000)_expression_pedal.jpg)

After recording automation using the mod wheel, you will see an automation curve, similar to the one shown in the following screenshot:

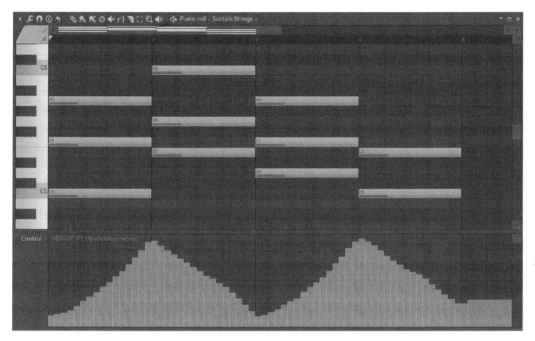

Figure 4.17 – Expression

Then, you can left-click the automation curve to refine the curve to your desired shape.

The Piano roll isn't just limited to automating expression and velocity. By left-clicking on the **Control** button at the bottom left of the Piano roll, you can swap between the parameters you wish to automate. For example, you can automate panning, volume, and pitch. Any effects that you control in the pattern will show up here. You can also use this menu to switch back to controlling note velocity.

The following screenshot shows the various channel controls:

Figure 4.18 – Choosing a parameter to automate

With that, you know how to use expression to add dynamic changes to your orchestral compositions. Next, we'll learn how to compose orchestral music using MIDI.

Orchestral MIDI programming

Let's get to the real meat and potatoes of this chapter: tips on composing for orchestral compositions. In the new few sections, we'll mostly focus on MIDI programming for string instruments. By learning how to compose for strings, you'll learn about lots of transferrable tools and techniques that can be applied to composing orchestral compositions regardless, of whether you're composing for string, woodwind, brass, or percussion instruments.

Becoming good at composing for strings will give you transferable skills to compose for many orchestral instruments. So, although I will talk specifically about strings, you'll find that these lessons carry over to other orchestral instruments too.

Composing for string instruments

When we talk about string orchestral instruments, we're referring to the contrabass, cello, viola, and first and second violins. Composers devote a lot of attention to the string section of an orchestra. String instruments present a lot of freedom in terms of what can be done. They are extremely expressive in sound, blend in well with other orchestral instruments, and have lots of different articulations to experiment with. It's an opportunity for composers to show off their skills.

When composing for string instruments, you'll come across the terms *double stops* and *divisi*, both of which we will look at in the following subsections.

Double stops

Double stops refer to playing two notes at the same time on a string instrument. There are also triple stops and quadruple stops. Playing more than two strings at a time is difficult because it's tricky to bow more than two strings simultaneously. It's difficult to get your fingers into a double stop and difficult to get out gracefully. If you give a piece of music to a string player and the score is filled with triple stops and quadruple stops, you may discover that you've given your musician an unplayable piece.

Double stops are not such a big deal in a full orchestra, though. This is because the orchestra can divide the notes among musicians. When given to an orchestra, melodies that would involve double, triple, and quadruple stops are often split into separate instruments for musicians to play.

Divisi

How do you avoid double stops? You use divisi. Dividing notes into separate instruments is called **divisi**. Divisi is not always the best choice in all situations. Divisi should be avoided in the first violin and bass. Divisi in the first violin can sound overly shrill and piercing. It's better to have divisi in the second violin.

Divisi in the bass should usually be avoided too. Divisi in the bass can result in overly muddy, crunchy notes that all mush together. For this reason, it's best to avoid chords in the low-end registers, such as on the contrabass. Divisi in string instruments usually works best in cellos, violas, and second violins.

In the majority of situations, you only need five-note voices for a nicely balanced chord, one for each string instrument – contrabass, cello, viola, first violin, and second violin. Usually, the two lowest voices on the cello and contrabass double each other, and or play the same note in different octave registers. This helps give the bass notes a bit of body. It's often best to avoid differing notes between the cello and the contrabass unless you intentionally want crunchy, muddy sounds.

After assigning a melody to an instrument with a thin sound, you may notice that the playback of the instrument sounds quite thin. In such a case, it helps to double the notes an octave apart (layer a note with another of the same pitch but an octave higher). This can help thicken the sound.

When you're composing for wind instruments, such as brass and woodwind instruments, it can be easy to forget that wind instruments have physical limitations, should a live musician play your piece. If a live musician plays your composition someday, they will need breaks to catch their breath. To solve this, leave rests in-between phrases so that your musicians can breathe.

String instrument considerations with vocals

In pop songs, you need to leave frequency space for the vocals. Identify notes and frequencies that have the same range that vocals reside in. Then, see whether a string instrument is competing with the vocal. If it is, consider transposing the string instrument up or down an octave. If it doesn't sound good once you've done this, you may want to consider swapping the notes with another string instrument that fits that register better.

The following screenshot shows an example of comparing frequencies from a string instrument with the frequencies of a vocal:

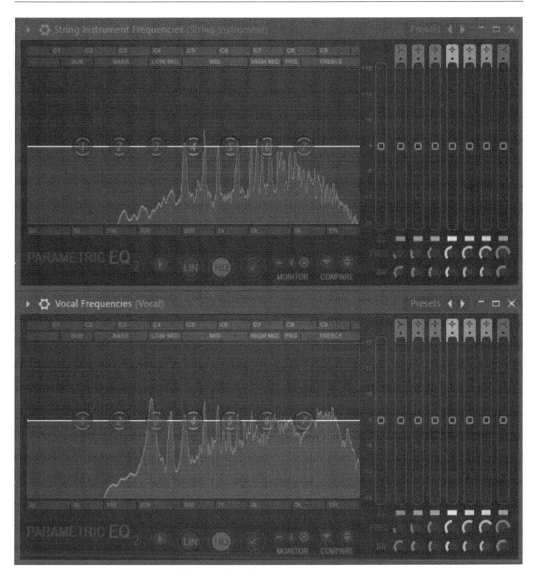

Figure 4.19 – Frequency comparison

In the preceding screenshot, we can see that the vocal occupies frequencies higher than 100 Hz. The string instrument occupies frequencies higher than 100 Hz. It's possible that in some situations, the frequencies from the string instrument may overpower the vocal since they are occupying the same frequency range. This may result in the vocal being drowned out.

Vocals are always the focus. Strings and other orchestral instruments are there to support the vocals. When you're creating counter-melodies with vocals, string instruments should occur when the vocals hold a note or take a break. When the vocal takes a break, the strings can take focus. When the vocal comes back in, the strings should have less movement so that they aren't distracting.

Tips for composing orchestral chord progressions

Is there just one way to start a chord progression? No. Any music theory book will tell you that. You could start with the bassline and build chords on top of that. You could start with a catchy melody and then build the bassline chords to support it. You could start with a rhythmic pattern first. You could search for the perfect sound that inspires you and build around the sound. There are many valid approaches, and you'll develop a preference that works best for you.

Saying you can make music in a lot of ways isn't very helpful, though. Let's assume that you took the first approach and built a bassline with your contrabass or another bass instrument. In this case, don't start building full chords right away. Building full chords from the start usually results in building very simple chords. Instead, once you have your bassline, you can add a single melody on top with another instrument such as the viola. You should layer your melodies on top of one another, making sure that each one improves the overall composition.

I come from a piano background. So, for me, the logical place to start is to improvise a chord progression on the piano. On the piano, the notes in the chords always end up being spaced close together. Why? Because my fingers are physically close to one another. If I were to swap the piano instrument with a string section, all my notes would probably be clumped together in just the viola or cello registers. It's easy to fix this issue, though – all I need to do is transpose notes in my chord progression up or down a few octaves to fit into the register of the violin, contrabass, and so on.

Can I have too many melodies?

When you have a bassline and a melody on top, how do you know whether it's safe to add another melody or when a new melody will distract from the overall effect?

In your melodies, you should have rests and places where your notes sustain for a while. It's during these pauses that you have the opportunity to introduce movement with a new melody. Movements that go up and down in pitch demand your attention. You want the focus to be on one melody at a time. In other words, when your viola holds a note or pauses, it's an opportunity for your second violin melody to take over with some melody movement.

When your second violin melody rests or holds a note, you can have your cellos do some movement. You want the focus to be on one melody at each point. When a melody reaches a logical hold or rest, shift the focus to another instrument. It's all about taking turns between active movement from one instrument section to the next. This way, the instruments feel like they're playing off each other. This example is a bit of an over simplification and I'm sure you can find exceptions. But its a useful way of thinking to keep in mind.

A good rule of thumb is that if you solo any instrument, the melody should sound interesting on its own. If not, you likely need to either improve the melody or add articulations to give it some more character.

If you choose to have clashing notes, such as a seventh note combined with a root note, it usually sounds better to have the clashing notes in the higher registers (above C3) rather than the lower registers. Anything in a register that's lower than C3 usually results in a muddy sound. In the higher registers, there's space for the clashing sounds, so they'll sound better than lower registers. The following screenshot shows two examples of seventh note partial chords. It's using notes C and B, which are being played by sustain string instruments.

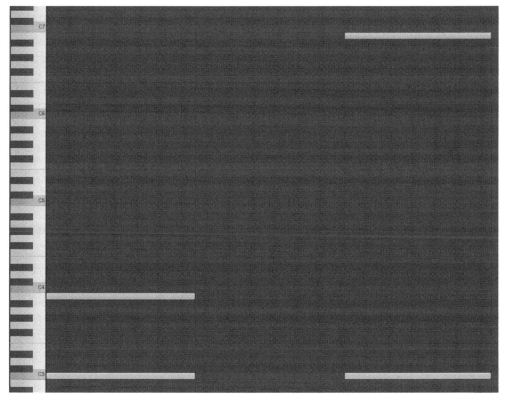

Figure 4.20 – Seventh note partial chords

The seventh note partial chord on the left is in the lower register. It sounds terrible to listen to as it's muddy and clashing. On the right, I've moved the seventh note up a few registers. This note, although still a seventh note, sounds much better. It has its own frequency space and doesn't feel like it's competing with the tonic note.

When transitioning from one sequence of block chords to the next, it's usually a good idea to have as little movement as possible between chords. Jumping up and down registers can sound jarring and should be avoided unless that's the intended effect. Instead, you want your chord progressions to be subtly expanding and contracting throughout the piece as you transition between chords.

Favor expanding and contracting chord progressions over linear vertical movements up and down. The following screenshot shows two examples of chord progressions:

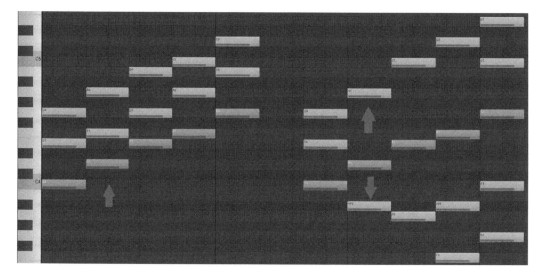

Figure 4.21 – Linear versus expanding chord progression

In the preceding screenshot, we can see an example of a mundane chord progression on the left and a more interesting chord progression on the right. I've used the same bassline for each in purple and added accompanying notes to form chords. On the left-hand side, we can see a linear vertical chord progression movement. All the notes are moving in the same direction. If you were to listen to this, it would sound boring and predictable.

On the right, we can see a chord progression where the overall movement of the chords expands up and down simultaneously. This is much more interesting to hear. An expansive or contractive movement in a chord progression is much more interesting to listen to than a linear movement.

Let's provide some general guidelines for orchestral composing. This order is a suggestion, so you will likely jump around these steps as you see fit:

1. Come up with basslines and add melodies to play over them, one at a time.

2. Spread your instrument voices out, assigning them to the logical string instrument registers – for example, high notes for the first violin and low notes for the contrabass and cello. You'll have to transpose up or down octaves based on what makes sense when you listen to it.

3. Brainstorm ways to add rhythm and movement to the composition. Experiment with rhythm syncopation to avoid sounding overly repetitive and predictable. Consider adding percussive elements to add syncopation and rhythm. Drum percussion is rarely a single instrument played in isolation. It's almost always a collection of layers of several percussive instruments playing simultaneously.

4. Add vertical movement to your melodies. If you find that a melody section is repetitive, consider jumping it up or down an octave. A downward movement in notes feels like it's losing energy, whereas an upward movement feels like it's gaining energy. Therefore, you will often see a downward movement in notes at the end of a chorus, when it's transitioning into a verse, and you'll often see an upward movement when it's transitioning into the chorus when we want higher energy.

5. Add rests and hold notes to add space to your melodies. This gives space for new melodies to be introduced for other instruments. Doing this makes your instruments sound like they're playing off one another.

6. Don't feel like you need all your instruments to be playing at all times. It's much more interesting to have instrument sections gradually fade in and out throughout the song. If you have all your instruments playing right at the start, you're depriving yourself of the chance to build up, layering all the instruments into a massive wall of sound crescendo later on.

7. Add articulations for your instruments.

8. Consider layering with additional orchestral instruments. For example, if you want your string instruments to have more attack, you may consider adding another string instrument with a punchier articulation, or a percussive instrument such as a xylophone. After layering, you may discover that some other orchestral instruments, such as brass or woodwind, fit in better than your original string instruments, so you'll need to do some swapping around.

9. Once you've added your articulations and layering, you can think about dynamics. It's a good idea to leave this until the end because any automation will need to be redone if you move your notes around. Refine the velocity of your notes and add expression to your instruments. Finally, add crescendos and decrescendos.

10. Balance the volume levels between your instruments. **EQ (equalize)** your instrument frequencies to give space for each instrument and focus attention on the main melody. Use automation so that your volume levels and/or expression change desirably throughout the song.

11. In some situations, you may consider swapping out the contrabass with a synthetic bass to hit the low frequencies. If you want to create what's known as a *wall of sound*, this is a way to hit the low resonating rumbly frequencies. If so, you will want to add a low pass filter for your synth bass instrument. By doing this, your synth bass frequencies focus on the low end and don't overpower the rest of your mix.

Tips for making sampled instruments sound realistic

To make your MIDI notes sound more like live string instruments, you may want to consider the following tips:

- Sample libraries don't know when a note is going to end. Real musicians get ready to come off of notes and have a natural decrescendo. You can attempt to mimic the decrescendo by automating expression.

- When a live orchestra begins playing a note, there's a slight crescendo when they start – a slight swell. Good sample libraries usually do this for you, but if you're using a cheap sample library, then you may have to find a workaround to make this happen.

- When real musicians play, their notes aren't exactly 100% in time. Naturally, there are some random fluctuations. You may be tempted to quantize everything with MIDI programming to get everything timed perfectly. Quantizing is a Piano roll effect that shifts notes to fit in with the Piano roll grid and removes any imprecision. Although this snaps everything to the Piano roll grid, it also makes everything overly robotically perfect. You can try to fix this by using an effect called **Humanize**, which exists on some digital audio workstations such as **Cubase**.

   Humanize adds a little random variation to the start and end times of your notes. FL Studio doesn't have a **Humanize** effect, so you'll have to go in and manually adjust the start and end times of your notes if you want to add some random variation.

   It's a lot of work trying to randomize by hand and even if you have a Humanize effect tool, it can still sound like it's lacking the realism of a live player. For this reason, high-level composers usually record their MIDI piano playing live and keep the timing of their playing with slight modifications. They also record their expression while playing, as opposed to going in and adding expression afterward. They do this using the mod wheel or a MIDI keyboard pedal.

- If all the note velocities are the same, your music will sound robotic. It's a good idea to add randomness to your note velocities to make them sound more like live instruments. For percussive instruments (especially drums), you should always be adding some velocity variation.

Adding random variation to your note velocities

FL Studio lets you add random variations to your note velocities. This can be done using a tool called the **Randomizer**. Let's learn how to use the Randomizer to add randomness to note velocities:

1. In the Piano roll, select the **Piano roll options | Tools | Randomize** dropdown, as shown in the following screenshot:

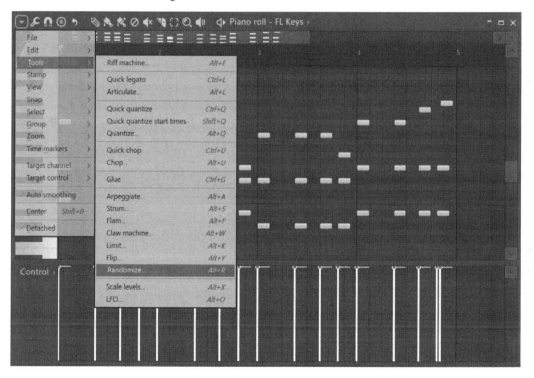

Figure 4.22 – Randomize

2. Disable the **Pattern** and **Bipolar** buttons. Adjust the velocity (**VEL**) knob to your velocity preference, as shown in the following screenshot:

Figure 4.23 – Randomizing velocity

3. After adjusting the knob, you'll find that the notes in your composition have been assigned some randomness to their note velocity. You may also want to randomize the panning and pitch.

With that, you know how to make your orchestral MIDI notes sound more realistic.

Considerations for mixing orchestral compositions

When mixing, you strive to achieve a nice balance between the low, mid, and high frequencies. This means you need to be careful when you're choosing instruments. Your note choice will also dictate whether you can achieve a nice balance. For example, the bass should rarely lie more than an octave from the part above it. Anything much more and you'll find that you're lacking in the mid frequencies. This is the reason why you should usually focus on five voices in the string section (one for each section – contrabass, cello, viola, first violin, and second violin). Achieving a good composition of these five voices will give you a nice balance of lows, mids, and highs.

Fortunately, in digital audio workstations, we have fine control over our sounds and can create combinations of sound that would be very difficult to achieve in the real world. We can use a tool for this called **equalization** (**EQ**). If an instrument is being drowned out, we can use EQ to carve out frequencies to enhance our instruments. For example, we can make cuts to frequencies to leave room for other instruments or boost frequencies that are too soft.

Reverb is an effect that simulates natural-sounding echoes in a space. When you're mixing sampled instruments, adding reverb effects can help blend your orchestral instruments. It makes it sound like all the instruments exist in the same room. Reverb often disappears behind the dialog when music is played at a low volume, so you can usually add quite a bit of reverb.

> **Tip**
>
> Turn your speakers down until you just barely hear the music and see whether it still sounds like it needs reverb.

For percussive instruments such as piano, harp, or percussion, a slight delay effect can help bring it to life.

When you're adding EQ, it's often a good idea to roll off the bottom and top frequencies of your instruments if you have poorly sampled instruments. This isn't necessary if you have good, sampled libraries.

At a pro level, composers don't use key switches for their instrument plugins. Key switches can become cumbersome when carrying out finely-tuned mixing for instrument articulations when they are frequently changing articulations. Doing so would require you to change your automation effects when you want to rearrange your note positioning. It's much easier to assign articulations to different instruments and mix them individually. Also, if you want to layer in instruments from different sample libraries, key switching makes it hard to keep track of where an articulation begins and ends.

When you're listening to your composition, you may notice some instruments overpowering others before you mix. With live orchestras, composers must account for what instruments can be layered together. If the wrong combination of instruments is paired up, some instruments may be drowned out entirely.

Understanding instrument frequency ranges can give you an idea of how to balance out your instruments so that you can achieve the desired sound. The following diagram shows the frequency ranges for instruments:

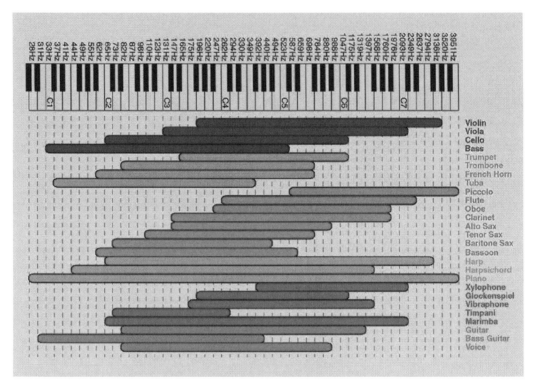

Figure 4.24 – Instrument frequency chart
(https://commons.wikimedia.org/wiki/File:Estensione_Strumenti_Musicale.jpg)

If you find that most of your instruments are occupying the same frequency range, you may find your instruments drowning each other out. In this case, it's worth swapping an instrument for one in a different frequency range.

While you're listening to your compositions, you can use plugins to visually see the frequency ranges in your mixer channels. If you can, you may want to look into spectrogram plugins. Spectrogram plugins provide you with a fine-grained insight into your song's frequencies.

Considerations for live orchestras

Why do we use live orchestras if plugin sample libraries are so good? Live orchestras have a few advantages over sampled orchestra plugins. In live orchestras, you have access to much more natural-sounding articulations. For example, when you play a sustain instrument sample, your digital audio workstation doesn't know when you plan to stop playing the note. So, it just loops the sample and then abruptly ends. When a real player plays a sustained note, the musician can make the sound flow in and out of the note naturally.

Live musicians can get ready to play the note before it begins and get ready to end the note before it ends with a decrescendo. Note that the top-of-the-line sample libraries are getting good at trying to make this sound natural, so this is becoming less and less of an issue.

Another reason you should use live orchestras is due to recording through microphones. When you record an orchestra, you have close microphones (called **tree mics**), microphones that are further away (called **wide mics**), and microphones to capture the whole room, including reverb (called **surround mics**). When the orchestra plays, your tree mics capture some of the orchestral instruments next to them.

Parts of other orchestra instruments will bleed into each tree mic recording. This makes it sound natural. When you use a sample library, you don't get the sound of all the instruments blending into each other naturally. Try adding a reverb effect to place all your orchestral instruments in a simulated room to mimic this behavior.

Now that we've learned how to compose orchestral compositions, let's summarize this chapter.

Summary

The ability to compose for orchestra is highly valued when composing for films and video games. Understanding orchestral MIDI composing techniques lets you quickly compose orchestral music and deliver scores to be played by live musicians.

In this chapter, you learned how to create orchestral music using MIDI programming. You learned about the various plugins you can use to create orchestral music. You also learned how to use velocity, articulations, and expression to add realism to your compositions. Finally, you learned about various orchestral MIDI programming techniques, tips for making sampled instruments sound real, and mixing ideas.

In the next chapter, you'll learn how to create sheet music for musicians, sync music to visuals, and also how to create sound effects.

Part 3: Designing Music for Films and Video Games

In this section, you will learn the ins and outs of composing for specific mediums and genres. You will learn techniques for composing for films and video games. You will also learn how to trigger specific emotions with music. Finally, templates are provided to guide you through your first soundtrack project.

We will cover the following chapters in this section:

- *Chapter 5, Creating Sheet Music with MuseScore, Scoring with Fruity Video Player, and Diegetic Music*

- *Chapter 6, Influencing Mood with Music and Designing Emotional Music*

- *Chapter 7, Creating Interactive Music for Video Games with Wwise*

- *Chapter 8, Soundtrack Composing Templates*

5

Creating Sheet Music with MuseScore, Scoring with Fruity Video Player, and Diegetic Music

As a composer, there are a few tool skillsets you should have. One of these is creating sheet music for live musicians. Doing this requires familiarity with music notation software. One of the most popular ones is **MuseScore**. Using MuseScore, you can export your music project and quickly generate sheet music with ease.

You should be able to sync music to visuals. A director will request that your music hits certain marks and you should know how to time your music to do so. This can be done using a video plugin in your digital audio workstation. In this chapter, we'll learn how to sync audio to visuals using the FL Studio Fruity Video Player tool.

While composing for projects of any visual medium, you should consider how sound effects fit into the picture. Expect some jobs to focus less on the music and more on developing sound effects. If you take a step back and look at sound for films and games from a high level, you could think of music as just a type of sound effect. Your job is to create the sound that fits the picture. It doesn't have to be music in the traditional sense. You should be ready to create whatever sound is necessary to make your visuals come alive.

In this chapter, we'll cover the following topics:

- Creating sheet music in MuseScore from an FL Studio project
- Syncing music to visuals using Fruity Video Player
- Diegetic music (The Art of Foley) and sound effects
- Recommended sound effect plugins

Creating sheet music in MuseScore from an FL Studio project

Sheet music is printed music with music notation. It contains information about note choice and placement. By reading sheet music, musicians recreate the song. You can include lots of information in sheet music, such as the notes used, articulations, volume changes, and time signatures. The more detailed the sheet music, the more direction you give the musician playing your piece.

Throughout most of musical history, songs have been passed down from one generation to another using only sheet music. Without sheet music, songs would be forgotten. If you learn how to play a live instrument, you will also need to learn how to read sheet music in order to play songs.

In this section, we'll learn how to create sheet music using MuseScore. This will allow live musicians to look at your compositions and know how to play them. If you plan on recording music for live musicians, you need to be ready to quickly translate your music into sheet music at a moment's notice. **MuseScore** is music notation software created for this purpose. It's free, open source, and very importantly, allows you to easily import MIDI data, which is what you create in digital audio workstations. Importing MIDI data makes it super easy to create sheet music.

MuseScore can also give you access to hundreds of thousands of sheet music scores for songs. This is very convenient when learning how to play music created by fellow musicians or composers. If you google a popular song's MIDI file and download it, you can import the MIDI file into MuseScore.

You can download MuseScore for free at `https://musescore.org/`. The following screenshot shows the MuseScore website's home page where you can download the software:

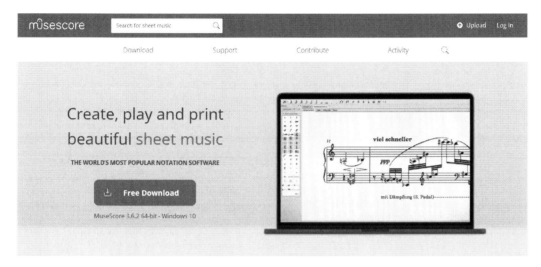

Figure 5.1 – MuseScore website

After downloading, when you first open MuseScore, you'll be greeted with an empty sheet music project. The following screenshot shows MuseScore when you open a new project:

Figure 5.2 – MuseScore new project

Starting a new project is okay, assuming you want to be composing your entire song from scratch, but that's not a very efficient way to compose. We're going to learn a much faster, and easier, approach. We'll take our entire FL Studio composition and then transfer it over to MuseScore. Essentially, we're doing the equivalent of copying and pasting MIDI music notes so that MuseScore can do most of the music notation work for us. This will save you a tremendous amount of time.

Frankly, I was blown away the first time I saw how easy the following technique is. Perhaps you will be too. Here's how to create sheet music with MuseScore using a project from FL Studio:

1. Download and install MuseScore.

2. Create a song in FL Studio.

    To execute the following steps, you need a song in FL Studio to export as MIDI data. You can use any song you've created in FL Studio as long as it uses some MIDI notes in the Piano roll.

3. We're about to export your project as MIDI data. Before that, make sure you save a copy of your project as a backup. Preparing your project for MIDI exporting will irreversibly modify your project. Therefore, you must save a backup copy first so that you have access to the original in case you want to make further adjustments.

4. Make sure all your instruments in the Channel rack are appropriately named. MuseScore will label each section based on the instrument name you set up in the Channel rack.

    You can rename instruments by right-clicking **Rename, color and icon...** on an instrument in the Channel rack, as shown in the following screenshot:

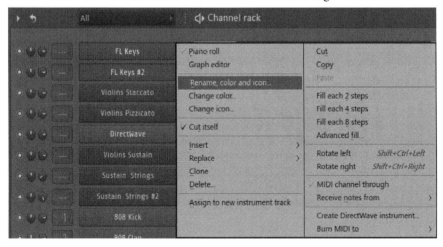

Figure 5.3 – Naming your instruments prior to exporting

Make sure you give your instruments names that are easily recognizable later on.

5.   In FL Studio, navigate to **Tools | Macros | Prepare for MIDI export**, as shown in the following screenshot:

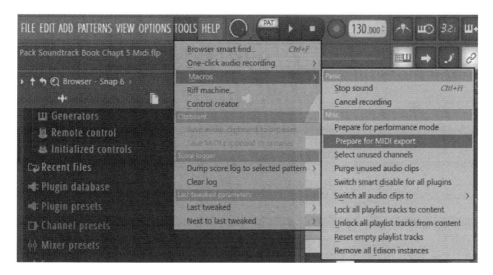

Figure 5.4 – Prepare for MIDI export

After selecting **Prepare for MIDI export**, a series of steps will be performed on your project to prepare for MIDI exporting.

6.   Navigate to **FILE | Export | MIDI File**. A pop-up window will appear prompting you to save your MIDI file and give it a name. Remember where you save your MIDI file.

7. Make sure that **MID** is selected and then click **Start**, as shown in the following screenshot:

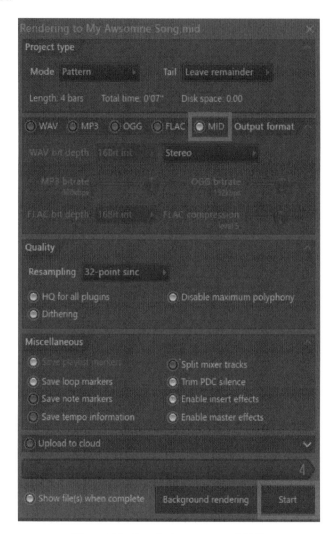

Figure 5.5 – Rendering a song as MIDI

Your song has been rendered as a MIDI file. We can now import this into MuseScore.

8. Open up MuseScore.

9. Select **Load score from file** and select the MIDI file you exported from FL Studio. The following screenshot shows how you can import your project:

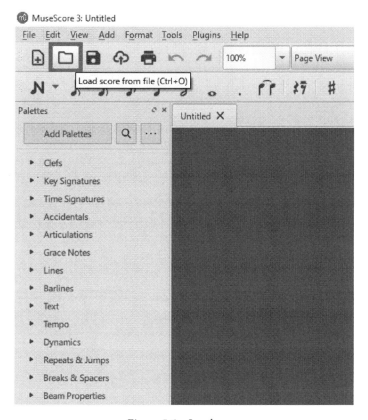

Figure 5.6 – Load score

After selecting your MIDI file, MuseScore will populate a score using data from the MIDI file. The following screenshot shows the sheet music that MuseScore generated from an FL Studio project:

Figure 5.7 – MuseScore adding your song

Wow! That was easy. We didn't have to worry about figuring out the note placement and spacing at all.

You'll notice that MuseScore made some mistakes. For example, it made assumptions about the naming of instruments that may or may not be correct. You'll need to go and fix those in MuseScore afterward. Also, MuseScore can import notes but doesn't know how to import articulations directly from the digital audio workstation. For that, you'll need to go and manually add in music notation.

Not to worry, there are plenty of tools for adding sheet music details such as titles, tempo, key signatures, and articulations. On the left-hand side of MuseScore, you'll see a list of palettes with music notation.

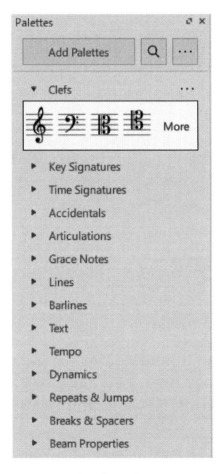

Figure 5.8 – Palette list with music notation

By left-clicking on any of the palette drop-down arrows, you can see a list of available notations. You can then left-click and drag a notation onto your sheet music.

Adding music notation is very easy; just grab the item that you need from the left-hand side palettes and drag them onto your score. It's very intuitive.

Congratulations! You now know how to export your project from FL Studio to MuseScore to create sheet music. Next, let's learn how to sync music to visuals with Fruity Video Player.

Syncing music to visuals using Fruity Video Player

If you're brought onto a film production team early, the director may ask you to compose a song with key emotions necessary for the scene before it's filmed. You'll compose the song, and the editor adjusts the footage to fit the song whenever the footage is ready. This is the easiest scenario for you. It allows you lots of flexibility and freedom to experiment with minimal restrictions. If scoring for animation, music is almost always composed before the animating stage, meaning animators can design around the music.

Music does not always come before visuals though. This is especially true if you are brought in to score footage in postproduction. There are situations where the director will give you an edited cut of the film and tell you to score your music based on the footage. If the director disliked the music composed by a previous composer, it means you'll need to come in and either fix or rescore the film.

If the video footage already exists, you'll need to adjust your music to hit certain key moments in the film, adapting it to hit key timings demanded by the visuals. FL Studio offers tools designed to map out your music timings and sync music to video.

The tool in FL Studio that syncs music to video is called **Fruity Video Player**. Fruity Video Player comes with FL Studio version Signature Edition and up.

Let's start scoring with Fruity Video Player:

1.   In the Channel rack, right-click on an instrument and select **Insert | Fruity Video Player**.

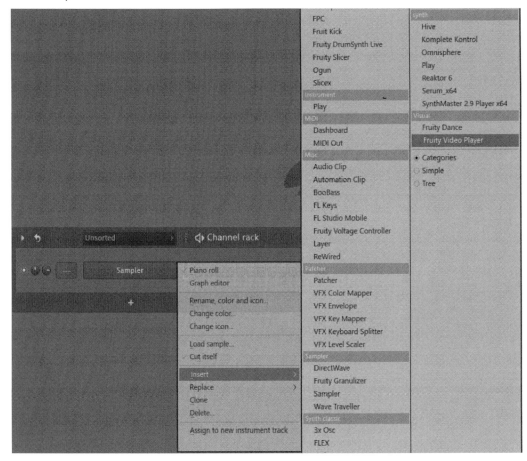

Figure 5.9 – Inserting Fruity Video Player

The plugin will load up and you'll see the following:

Figure 5.10 – Fruity Video Player

Fruity Video Player allows you to load in videos to play in sync with visuals.

2. Clicking outside of the plugin can cause it to become hidden by background panels. This is annoying since you usually want the video player to always be visible. We can fix this by clicking the drop-down plugin option and selecting **Detached**, as shown in the following screenshot:

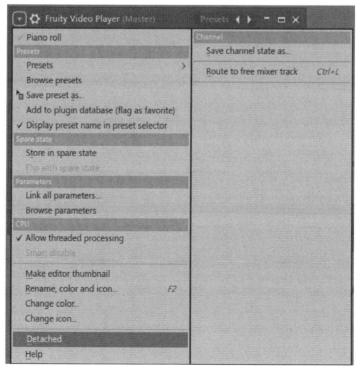

Figure 5.11 – Detaching Fruity Video Player

From now on, Fruity Video Player will remain in the foreground at all times.

3.   Load a video into the player by clicking the **Load video file…** button (the button on the left side that looks like a folder) and choosing a video of your choice on your computer. The video will be loaded into the player. You can now play the video in FL Studio.

4.   In the plugin options dropdown, you'll see several other tools available, as shown in the following screenshot:

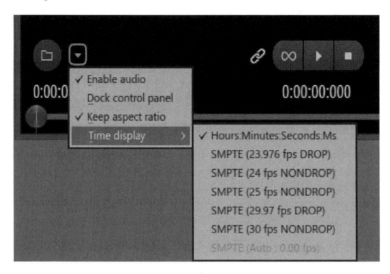

Figure 5.12 – Plugin options

We get the following plugin options after clicking on the drop-down arrow:

- **Enable audio**: Can be disabled to save CPU power.

- **Dock control panel**: Keeps the controls over the video. When deselected, the controls appear when the mouse hovers over them.

- **Keep aspect ratio**: Keeps the video aspect ratio. If deselected, rescaling the video player will rescale the size of the video.

- **Time display**: Set the information shown in the last three digits of the time display (milliseconds (ms) or **Society of Motion Picture and Television Engineers (SMTPE)** format). The video you're scoring may have a different time format so you may need to adjust this to fit your video.

- **Slave Playback To Host**: As shown in the following screenshot, this syncs your playlist music to the playback of the video:

Figure 5.13 – Slave Playback to Host

If not selected, the video will play independently of the song in the playlist. You'll usually want this to be selected.

- The **as start time** and **as end time** buttons let you set when you want the video to begin and end playing. The following screenshot shows the **as start time** and **as end time** buttons:

Figure 5.14 – The as start time and as end time buttons

You might want to use these if you need to start scoring a few seconds into the video instead of exactly at the start.

We have our video player loaded up. Now we need to learn how to map out our visuals in FL Studio and label important moments. Visual labels will make it easier to hit precise music timings. We do this by setting markers.

Setting markers

Markers are useful for giving you a visual reference for moments you need your music to hit. Markers are visual label indicators you can manually set in your playlist timeline. For example, perhaps you need your music to come in or fade out at a certain timed position. Markers can help you to identify where the position is.

Let's learn how to create markers:

1. Load an instance of Fruity Video Player into the Channel rack. Load a video into Fruity Video Player that you want to score music for.

2. Make sure that Fruity Video Player is detached so it remains open when you click outside of the player window.

3. Set the in and out points of the video using the **as start time** and **as end time** controls.

4. Ensure that **Slave Playback To Host** is enabled so that your video is synchronized to the playlist.

5. Open the playlist.

6. Create a new empty pattern in the playlist and make it as long as the video you want to score. If your video is 1 minute long, make sure the pattern in the playlist is also 1 minute long.

In the following screenshot, you can see I've created a new pattern called **My Video** in the playlist:

Figure 5.15 – Empty pattern added to the playlist

7. Scroll through your playlist timeline. You can do this by left-clicking on the timeline and dragging your cursor left or right. As you drag, the video in Fruity Video Player will move in sync according to the position in the timeline. An example of the cursor being dragged is shown in the following screenshot:

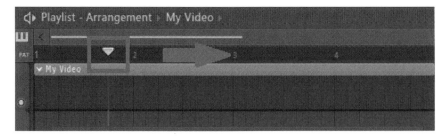

Figure 5.16 – Dragging along the timeline

8. While scrolling through the timeline, when you reach a scenic moment of importance, press *Ctrl + T*. Doing this will create a marker on the timeline with the name **Auto**.

9. Right-click on the marker and rename it with a meaningful name of your choice. The following screenshot shows an example:

Figure 5.17 – Added marker

10. Repeat this process for all key moments throughout your video.

Go through any notes you collected when you were interviewing the film director. The director will have a vision of what emotions they want in any given scene. There should be cues for when intensity should increase or die down, and when the director wants music to come in or out. You can add visual markers for all of these cues throughout your video.

The following screenshot shows an example of markers set for important moments in the video:

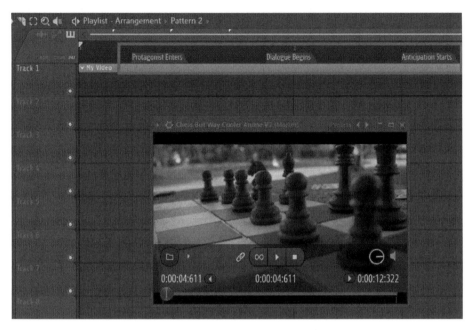

Figure 5.18 – Markers set in the video

By setting markers in your video, you can visualize all of the important changes that need to occur in your music. This will help you to plan out your music.

> **Note**
> Markers can be set in the playlist or in the Piano roll. Often, it is helpful to set markers in the Piano roll so you can see where your MIDI note placement aligns.

Setting time signatures

Time signatures allow you to organize and measure music. They divide it into beats per bar of music to make it easier to read and understand. It's a little like how you have periods at the end of sentences to distinguish one sentence from the next. They help to give structure to written music.

Time signatures consist of a top and bottom number. By default, FL Studio projects load projects with a time signature of 4/4. This means 4 beats per bar of music. In the Piano roll, this means the grid is divided into 16 squares. The following screenshot shows an example with one bar of music. You'll see 16 boxes horizontally lined up in the bar.

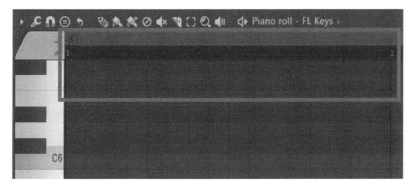

Figure 5.19 – 4/4 time signature

Music isn't confined to 4/4 time signatures, many songs are in different time signatures. Using a different time signature allows you to create different styles of music. For example, songs in the style of a waltz have the time signature of 3/4 instead of 4/4.

You can change the time signature of your song. Changing time signatures is done the same way you add markers to your song.

Let's change the time signature of a song:

1. Identify a location in a Piano roll pattern where you want to change the time signature.

2. Press *Ctrl + T* on your keyboard. A marker will show up on the timeline at the cursor position.

3. Right click on the newly created marker. Choose the **Add time signature** option. An example is shown in the following screenshot:

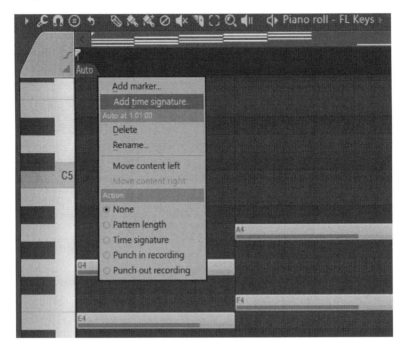

Figure 5.20 – Add time signature

A window will pop up, allowing you to select the time signature you want. **Numerator** is the beats, and **Denominator** is the bar. By default, it is 4/4 (meaning 4 beats per bar). The following screenshot shows an example:

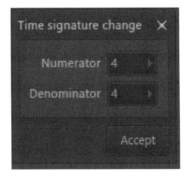

Figure 5.21 – Time signature change

4. Change the time signature values to ones of your choosing. You can add markers throughout your song with varying time signatures. The following screenshot shows an example:

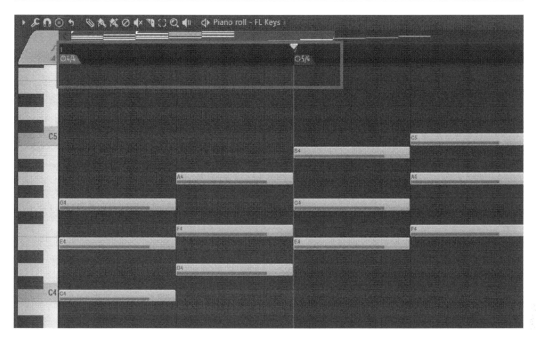

Figure 5.22 – Time signature changes throughout the song

You now know how to change time signatures throughout your song. Changing time signatures allows you the freedom to shift different styles of music throughout your piece.

We've learned how to sync music to video using Fruity Video Player. Next, let's discuss diegetic music and sound effects.

Diegetic music (The Art of Foley) and sound effects

In the 1920s, Jack Foley became famous for adding sound effects to stories told over the radio. Over time, adding sound effects to the narrative became known as the **Art of Foley**. You may have also come across the term *diegetic sound*, which is the same thing. **Diegetic** sound is any sound that emanates from the story world of the film.

Except for dialog, most of what you hear when you watch a movie wasn't recorded at the time the visual was filmed. Every explosion, footstep, weather sound, movement, animal growl, and other sound effects are sounds that have been carefully designed and chosen after the footage was recorded.

If sound effects are done right, the audience won't notice the film is filled with sounds added in post-production. Excellent sound design matches the visuals with the sound seamlessly, so your mind thinks they were created together.

All sound involves two elements hitting one another in some fashion. What sound it creates depends on the material and method of making them collide. Large studios hire Foley artists to go through their films and strategically add sounds for every item. In other words, people smack things together and record the sound they make.

As audience members, we take sound effects for granted. As sound designers, sound effects are not quite so obvious. Creating sound involves care and thought being put into each sound.

When composing, it's important to consider what sounds the director intends to place in the film. Sound effects often take the focus away from the music. If you're in a scene with lots of very overpowering sound effects, you'll want to consider the effect this has on the music as it may get hidden behind the sound effects.

Diegetic music involves taking sounds that emanate from the story and using them as your instruments when composing music. These sounds may or may not be orchestral instruments – they could be any sound effects. The benefit of composing diegetic music as opposed to using regular instruments is that it helps the music to feel connected to the world of the visuals.

Although diegetic music is only sometimes done in scoring for film, it is done all the time when scoring music for video games. The sound effects and music for video games often blend together so seamlessly that you forget where one begins and the other ends.

We'll explore scoring music for video games in much more detail in *Chapter 7, Creating Interactive Music for Video Games with Wwise*.

Sound effect examples

Let's consider some examples of sound effects used in films. In the movie *Fight Club*, there are lots of hand-to-hand combat sounds. The sounds of bone-crunching punches were created by smashing chicken drumsticks and recording the sounds. The sound of roaring waves in films is often created by recording the sound of a sheet of vibrating metal. And the sound of snow in films is usually the sound of someone stepping on sand. Crunching snow sounds are often actually the sound of cornstarch being crunched.

Here are some recommended videos showing how sound effects are created for films:

- **Fight Club | The Beauty of Sound Design**: `https://youtu.be/as2Rk4WcljA`
- **The Magic of Making Sound**: `https://youtu.be/UO3N_PRIgX0`

Adding sound effects is usually done in video editing software rather than a digital audio workstation. This is so you can get the timings precisely synced with the visuals. Syncing sound effects can be done in a digital audio workstation, but it's usually easier in video editing software.

Recommended sound effect plugins

Although you can go out and create sound effects for your project, it may be worth investigating whether there are already existing sound libraries and tools that meet your requirements, especially if you're working to a deadline. There are also lots of websites that offer sound effects intended for films.

Let's discuss a few cutting-edge sound effect plugins. **Krotos** creates plugins for sound design. Krotos's plugins are used in many film productions and are available at `https://www.krotosaudio.com/`.

Dehumaniser

Krotos's **Dehumaniser** is their most famous audio effect plugin. It works by modifying vocals to create monster sounds. It has been used in films such as *Avengers: Age of Ultron*, *The Jungle Book*, *The Conjuring*, and the series such as *Stranger Things*. The following screenshot shows the Dehumaniser plugin:

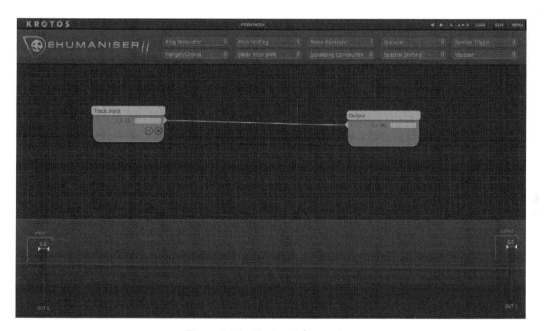

Figure 5.23 – Krotos Dehumaniser

Functioning like a vocoder plugin, it takes a vocal input and modifies the sound to create a voice of your choosing. Saying Dehumaniser is like a vocoder is a bit of an understatement though as this plugin can turn your voice into an animal growl or a Transformers robot.

You can learn more about Dehumaniser at `https://www.krotosaudio.com/dehumaniser2/`.

Igniter

Krotos's **Igniter** plugin allows you to create the sounds of vehicles, sports cars, motorbikes, planes, helicopters, spacecraft, drones, and many other vehicles.

Figure 5.24 – Krotos Igniter

It includes the sounds of cars, planes, helicopters, motorcycles, trucks, and tractors. Here's a list of some of the vehicle sounds included:

Agusta Westland 119x, Aston Martin, Rapide, Audi R8, BMW i3, Bucker BU 131, Cessna 560XL, CH-47D Chinook, Dacia 1310, De Havilland Tiger Moth, Ferrari 348, Ford F150, Harley Davidson 99 Hog, Honda Civic, Huey UH-1H, Land Rover Defender, Mercedes Actros, Porsche Carrera, Subaru Crosstrek SUV, Agusta Westland, Tesla Model S, Toyota Chaser, U650M Tractor, and Subaru Impreza

You can learn more about Igniter at `https://www.krotosaudio.com/igniter/`.

Reformer

Krotos's **Reformer** plugin creates Foley sounds in a dynamic way. It allows you to create real-time synced sound effects for visuals.

Figure 5.25 – Krotos Reformer

Modifying the Reformer controls in real time creates a new sound. Its most obvious application is for creating sounds for animations that have no existing sound to begin with so you need to invent something from scratch. For example, it can be used to create sounds for animations where you need a new sound to be a custom length.

You can learn more about Reformer at `https://www.krotosaudio.com/reformer-pro/`.

Weaponiser

Krotos's **Weaponiser** allows you to create sound effects for weapons. The following screenshot shows the Weaponiser plugin:

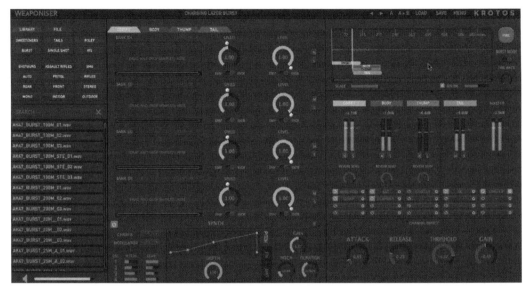

Figure 5.26 – Krotos Weaponiser

Weaponiser allows you to quickly come up with sounds for real and sci-fi weapons, sci-fi sound effects, footsteps, whooshes, and transitions and customize them for any given situation.

You can learn more about Weaponiser at `https://www.krotosaudio.com/ weaponiser/`.

Omnisphere

Spectrasonics **Omnisphere** is a well-known synthesizer. It's a MIDI plugin with a vast repertoire of sampled unique instruments perfect for sound design.

Figure 5.27 – Spectrasonics Omnisphere

Omnisphere is massive. It offers thousands of sampled live instruments and synthesizers. It can import sounds and modulate and apply effects to them. It's a beast of a plugin.

You can learn more about Omnisphere at `https://www.spectrasonics.net/products/omnisphere/`.

Sound effect libraries

If you don't have time to modify and customize sound effects yourself, you might consider getting access to royalty-free sound effects libraries. There are lots of websites selling SFX (sound effects). These websites offer thousands of royalty-free audio samples.

Some websites sell individual samples as a package, while others sell a subscription allowing you to gain access to their entire library for an annual fee. You can then simply download and use the audio any way you like.

Websites that provide sound effects include the following:

- **Boom Library**: `https://www.boomlibrary.com/`

- **ProSoundEffects**: `https://www.prosoundeffects.com/`

- **Sound Ideas**: `https://www.sound-ideas.com/`

- **Artlist**: `https://artlist.io/sfx/`
- **Soundsnap**: `https://www.soundsnap.com/`
- **Soundly**: `https://getsoundly.com/`

Diegetic music and sounds can make an audience feel like they're experiencing a real event. If done carefully, sounds can draw an audience in, so they think sound emanates from the story itself. The tools and resources you learned about in this section will get you up and creating feature film-ready sound effects.

Summary

In this chapter, we learned how to create sheet music in MuseScore. This lets you export your music out of FL Studio to give to live musicians to play.

We learned how to sync music to video using Fruity Video Player. This allows you to fine-tune your music timing so you can hit important key moments in your video.

Finally, we learned about diegetic music so that you can consider sound effects for your films and video games. We discussed recommended products and sound effect libraries to consider for your projects.

In the next chapter, we'll learn about creating adaptive music for video games.

6
Influencing Mood with Music and Designing Emotional Music

As a composer, you have the power to control the emotions of an audience. Visuals acquire different meanings depending on the audio used to accompany them. You can turn a boring scene where nothing happens into a powerful emotional moment simply by the selection of sound. You can make a scene happy or sad, relaxing or intense, or romantic or scary by the musical choices you make.

There are a few common emotions that come up again and again in films. In this chapter, we will touch on multiple tips and tricks to help you design musical moods for a variety of emotions.

In this chapter, we'll cover the following topics:

- What is fear?
- Designing a jump scare
- Designing creepy music
- Composing happy and sad music
- Composing romantic music
- Creating tension in music and composing epic music for trailers

If you're a beginner and you feel overwhelmed, take comfort in knowing you don't need to memorize the techniques discussed in this chapter. This chapter is intended to serve as a reference guide you can refer to whenever you need music in a specific mood. These techniques are tailored toward niche situations that occasionally come up.

In this chapter, we'll try to give you not only the tools to compose for specific moods but also the rationale behind why certain sounds cause you to feel a particular way. With this understanding, you'll gain the insight to experiment and come up with new sounds yourself.

Composing spooky music

Understanding how sound can be used to make your audience feel uncomfortable is a great tool available to the composer. If done correctly, music can simultaneously terrify your audience while keeping them thoroughly engaged and invested in the story. Before we can scare our audience, we need to understand what fear is.

What is fear?

Fear is a psychological response to the uncertainty of potential danger. From a biological perspective, fear helps you avoid situations that could harm you.

Let's think about your distant ancestors roaming around in the wild outdoors, back when they were hunting and foraging for food. In the darkness of forests or jungles, they couldn't see what was going on around them. Their ears were listening closely for sounds of creatures that could harm them.

The unknown is dangerous. Over thousands of years, our ears have become sensitive, distinguishing familiar sounds from the unfamiliar. Anything our ears interpret as a threat can cause our body to enter a state of heightened attention. Your body diverts blood to organs that help in a fight-or-flight scenario; your heart pounds, your ears listen intensely, and your eyes dart around. These are all survival mechanisms to give you a better chance of surviving when facing a potential threat. If we want to generate these biological responses with sound, we need to create a sensory environment to trick the listener into believing that they are in a dangerous scenario.

What sounds cause us to think that something might be dangerous? It's not that obvious at first glance. Note that there are different kinds of fear, too. Sometimes, we feel chills down our spine. Sometimes, we jump in fright from surprises. Sometimes, we see pictures that are unsettling and disturbing, but there isn't an obvious threat. How do we explain all of these different forms of fear? We need another piece of the psychological puzzle, and that piece is called **cognitive dissonance**.

Understanding cognitive dissonance

Cognitive dissonance is the perception of inconsistent or contradictory information. When you encounter inconsistent or contradictory information, your mind struggles to make sense of the information. In certain situations, it results in putting your body into a state of stress, and you experience fear.

We can create cognitive dissonance for our ears by combining sounds that don't sound like they'd naturally go with each other. By creating an auditory situation that is unfamiliar, we can make ourselves feel uncomfortable. Pair an unsettling sound with an unsettling visual and you have an excellent situation to spark fear in the heart of your audience.

Here's an example of cognitive dissonance:

Tense scene + innocent music = creepy

Your eyes see a scene that is very intense. Perhaps the actors look stressed out and are panicking. Now, layer that intense scene with the sound of something very innocent-sounding – it will conflict with the visual and create cognitive dissonance.

In many horror movies involving clowns, murderous child toys, or possessed children, you'll hear innocent music. It might involve the sounds of toys, carousel music, or children singing. If this sound accompanies a tense scene, it can be interpreted by the mind as creepy.

If you reverse the preceding equation, you can end up with a situation that can be interpreted as funny.

Innocent scene + tense music = funny

There's a scene in the film *Mr. Bean's Holiday* (`https://youtu.be/wUEYIhP_9ag`) that is a good example of an innocent scene with dramatic music, which comes across as funny. So, cognitive dissonance works well for creating fear and also humor.

So, fear is... what?

Fear is not the act of seeing danger head-on. Fear is the emotion you get when you aren't sure whether there is danger or not. It's a feeling of believing you are in a situation of danger. There's uncertainty, though, and this doubt causes you stress.

Seeing a menacing monster doesn't necessarily cause you fear if you see it coming from a mile away and you're well prepared to fend off the threat. Not knowing whether there is a threat nearby, what it might be, nor how close or how dangerous it is – that's significantly scarier and likely to induce a fearful emotion. In other words, the goal is to create scenarios of uncertainty in the mind of your listener.

Designing a jump scare

Most horror movies have a moment where something jumps out and a sound is used to heighten the emotion. This is called a **jump scare**.

The audience usually thinks a jump scare got them because of the visuals on screen. What they don't realize is most of the tension in a jump scare comes from the way the sound has built up to that moment. The scariest movie scenes are worked on by master composers experienced in techniques to scare the listener through sound. Music can turn a scene where nothing happens into a tense build-up of suspense that has the audience on the edge of their seats.

What is a jump scare?

Jump scares are quite easy to do. An effective jump scare is composed of the following pieces:

- *A build-up of creepy sounds.*
- *The sound quietens down to add suspense..*
- *A loud, startling, and scary noise.*

A jump scare is the pairing of music and visuals to create a moment of fear followed by a moment of shock. Sometimes, there is nothing at the end of the jump scare; instead, the viewer receives the anticipation of an impending jump scare followed by a moment of relief when they discover there's nothing jumping out at them.

A good jump scare is created by using the following technique. First, creepy music grows in intensity, preparing the scene for a shocking event. After the creepy music reaches its climax in intensity, there's a short moment of quiet for anticipation, followed by a loud scary sound that is dissonant or clashing. This ending sound is paired with a shocking visual.

I mentioned that there's a build-up of creepy music in the preceding paragraph. Whenever you hear a rising or falling of intensity in sound, this usually means that we're going to be using automation. We learned how to use automation to increase expression and volume in *Chapter 4, Orchestral MIDI Composing*. **Expression** is an effect used to adjust the intensity and volume of your music. The following screenshot shows an example:

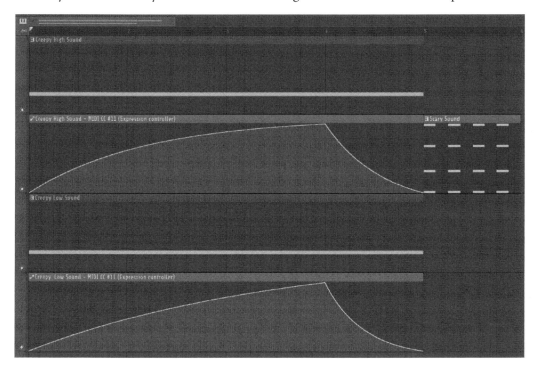

Figure 6.1 – Automating the intensity of creepy sounds

In the preceding screenshot, automation is used to increase the expression of an instrument's sound over time. Using automation, the intensity of the instrument's sound increases to a crescendo and then decreases to silence, followed by a scary sound.

Paired with an appropriate visual, the creepy sound builds up to a surprise reveal. We then decrease the intensity to silence for a moment. This serves to make the audience feel uncomfortable in anticipation of a jump scare, as the build-up they've experienced feels like it has to lead somewhere. Finally, we shock the audience with a scary sound and image combined, thus completing the jump scare.

Remember the order: *creepy music builds up, followed by silence for a few moments, and then a scary sound.* If you go straight to the scary sound, you're missing out on the build-up necessary to position your listener in a vulnerable state. The brief silence after the creepy music is a moment of suspense that's most important to scare your audience. The silence is a moment of uncertainty where the listener isn't sure what's going to happen next. If you hold the listener in a vulnerable state for a while, the fear builds up even more and the scene feels scarier.

Designing scary sounds

We've identified the key parts of a jump scare. It's made of **creepy music** followed by a **scary sound**. In the following pages, we'll diagnose how each of these is created. Let's start with the scary sound of the jump scare – the part that gives the final scare – and then we'll learn how to do **creepy music** after.

Scary sounds can be anything that sounds unfamiliar and unnatural – sounds that you don't commonly encounter in your everyday environment. There are several types of sounds that are good candidates for scaring your listener:

- **Frequency jumps**: Extreme frequency jumps can cause surprise to a listener. Frequency jumps are where you jump from a high frequency to a low frequency, or vice versa. Remember that frequency is just another word for pitch. In other words, we're saying any extreme changes in pitch. Extreme sudden jumps in pitch are uncommon in the everyday environment. There's usually a gradual rise or fall when going from high to low frequencies or vice versa.

  Using FL Studio, creating frequency jumps is very easy. It's just moving from notes in a high octave to notes in a low octave, or vice versa.

- **Nonstandard harmony**: Nonstandard harmonies are sounds that don't harmonize well – that is, sounds that are dissonant. If you have forgotten what dissonant sounds are, refer to *Chapter 3, Designing Music with Themes, Leitmotifs, and Scales.*

  Dissonant clashing sounds can be used to great effect. An iconic example is the dissonant screech of violins in Alfred Hitchcock's film *Psycho* during the murder scenes.

  The following shows an example of clashing notes that are very dissonant:

Figure 6.2 – Dissonant notes

Dissonant notes clash with each other and can be heightened even more by using a piercing instrument that sounds similar to a scream. In Alfred Hitchcock's film *Psycho*, the instrument used was a screeching violin.

- **Chaotic noise**: Chaotic sounds can create a situation where you feel panic and disorder. For example, if you pair a visual with the sound of a large angry crowd, shouting and disorderly running about, it can be interpreted as an overwhelming situation. Sounds similar to white noise can also feel very stressful and painful to listen to, which may be the desired effect in using them.

- **Sounds outside of the expected range**: Instruments are usually expected to play within a specific pitch range. If played outside of that range (be it higher or lower), they can sound very disconcerting. For example, if you have a recording of a human voice with the pitch decreased to an unnaturally low level, this can sound disturbing. The same can work for instruments too. Changing the pitch of an instrument to an unnaturally low or high level can sound very unnerving.

- **Sounds similar to a scream**: Our ears are highly tuned to hearing the sound of a scream. It's a biological safety mechanism with an evolutionary origin designed to alert us to danger, ensuring that when someone is screaming in fear, you pay attention to the source of the scream.

We've covered sounds that can be used to scare an audience in the "scare" part of a jump scare. Next, let's look at how to create creepy music for the build-up part of a jump scare.

Designing creepy music

Creepy music can be used in a variety of settings. Sometimes, you just need atmospheric sound to represent a certain environment or theme. If you want to add an air of mystery, suspense, or the feeling of the unknown, this is the section you're looking for.

Creepy music is made up of sounds that are unnatural and unfamiliar. The more out of the ordinary the sounds feel, the more likely they make good candidates for unnerving your audience.

In FL Studio, you can create sounds that will be interpreted as creepy by employing the following techniques:

- Detuning music
- Abruptly changing key midway
- Reversed music
- Slowing down, speeding up, and changing speed abruptly
- Reverb, glitches, and delay, which can be added to enhance any of the preceding methods

Detuned music

Most music is optimized to encourage notes that are in harmony with one another. Notes that are not in harmony with one another are known as *dissonant*. By contrast, the more harmonious sounds are, the more pleasing they are to the ears, and instruments are generally adjusted to be as in tune as possible. If you want to create sounds that are creepy, one approach you can take is to head in the exact opposite direction and devise instruments that are intentionally detuned. We covered consonance and dissonance in *Chapter 3, Designing Music with Themes, Leitmotifs, and Scales*.

Abruptly changing keys midway

Most songs maintain the same key throughout the song. This way, the music sounds consistent throughout. The music both sets and meets the listener's expectations of what sounds are likely to follow. If there is a transition from one key to another, we transition as smoothly as possible. When DJs play songs for a crowd, they arrange their song choices so that they are in similar keys when changing from one song to the next, making the transition feel less sudden and flow more naturally.

We learned how to transition between keys using the chord wheel technique, which we discussed in *Chapter 3, Designing Music with Themes, Leitmotifs, and Scales*.

If you want to send a jolt of surprise to your listener, you can change musical keys abruptly throughout your piece to keys that are dissimilar to one another. This sound is so unusual that your ears will focus on the change in key. This change can feel very unexpected and take a listener out of the moment. It's like breaking the fourth wall in a film where an actor looks directly into the camera at the audience. You make the audience aware that the music has completely changed. Abruptly changing tempo can also cause this effect on the listener.

Reversed music

As a general rule, sound plays in a forward direction. Playing sounds backward, especially if slowed down, can create some creepy and possibly horrific sounds. A popular game amongst vinyl record owners is to play famous songs in reverse, looking for hidden messages. This can result in some very strange and otherworldly sounds.

In FL Studio, you can reverse the sound of any sound sample by right-clicking twice on it in the playlist and then selecting the **Reverse** button. The following screenshot shows an example:

Figure 6.3 – Reversing an audio sample

If you want to make your sounds even creepier, you can consider slowing down the time and pitch of the audio as well.

Rendering audio to a wave form

If you have an instrument playing MIDI notes and you want to reverse the sound, you won't be able to simply double-click on the sample in the playlist. There's an additional step you need to do before you can reverse your sound. You need to convert the MIDI music notes to an audio waveform first. Once that is done, the sound becomes a regular audio sample, which you can reverse using the previously described method.

You can convert the instrument's MIDI note music to an audio sample using a technique called **rendering to audio**, more commonly known as **freezing audio**.

Let's learn how:

1. Route your instrument from the Channel rack to the Mixer. We learned how to do this in *Chapter 2, Navigating Through the Key Features of FL Studio*. The following screenshot shows an example:

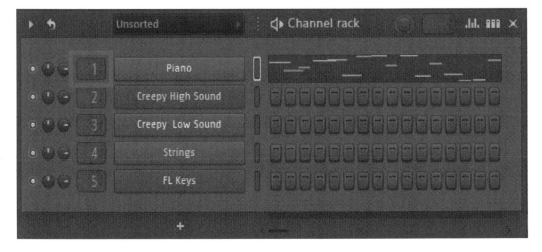

Figure 6.4 – Routing a Channel rack instrument to the Mixer

Here, you can see that I've routed my instruments in the Channel rack to the Mixer. I'll be converting the sound of the piano playing notes into an audio sample.

2. On the instrument for which you want to render the audio to a waveform, select the **Arm Disk Recording** button. You can select multiple tracks at once, as shown in the following screenshot:

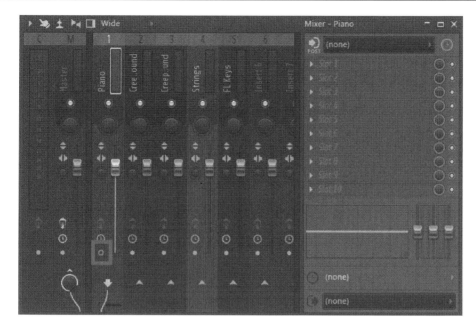

Figure 6.5 – Arm Disk Recording

3. In the Mixer, select **Options | Disk recording | Render to wave file(s)**, as shown in the following screenshot:

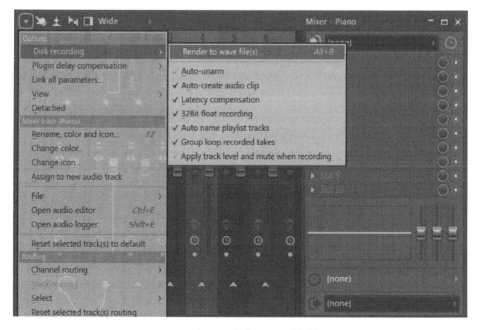

Figure 6.6 – The Render to wave file(s) option

A window menu with options will appear, as shown in the following screenshot:

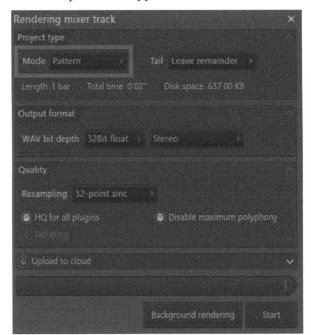

Figure 6.7 – The Rendering mixer track window

4. Adjust **Mode** to indicate whether you want to render your pattern or song. Pattern refers to a selected phrase of notes where as song refers to the entire composition.

5. Click **Start**. Your instrument in the Channel rack will play the MIDI notes and the Mixer will record the sound, creating an audio sample. This will then be outputted as a sample that can be placed in the Playlist:

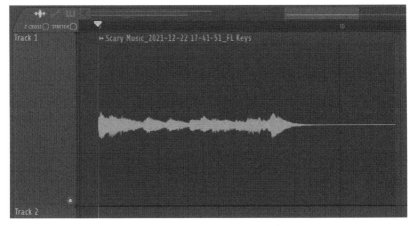

Figure 6.8 – The waveform is outputted

You can then double-click on the sample in the Playlist to gain access to the reverse sample controls:

Figure 6.9 – Reversing the rendered audio sample

Using the rendering-to-audio technique, you can convert any sound with or without effects in the Mixer into a sample and then reverse it.

Slowing down, speeding up, and changing speed abruptly

Changes in the speed of audio can be an unexpected event. Slowed-down music is often a very creepy sound, especially when accompanied by a decreasing pitch in the music.

Changing the speed of a sample is done differently than changing the speed of the entire song. If you want to change the speed of a sample and have it stay at the new speed, left-click twice on it and change the **PITCH** and **TIME** values as shown in the following screenshot:

Figure 6.10 – Changing the speed and pitch of a sample

This method changes the speed at a particular moment in the song. However, it doesn't automate a gradual change in the tempo and/or pitch of a sample over time.

If you want to change the speed over time, you need to change it for the entire project. You can do so by right-clicking on the project tempo and selecting **Create automation clip**.

This will allow you to adjust the tempo to speed the song up or slow it down, as shown in the following screenshot:

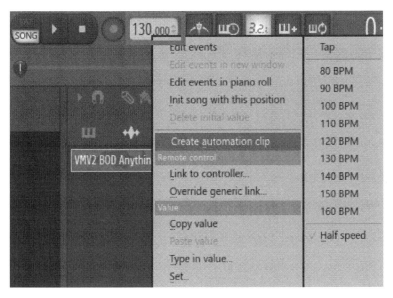

Figure 6.11 – Automating tempo

With automation, you can increase or decrease the tempo of your song over time, as shown in the following screenshot:

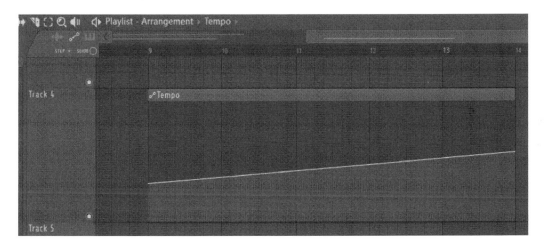

Figure 6.12 – Automating the tempo

In the preceding screenshot, we can see the tempo of the song increase in speed over time. You can also automate to do the opposite and have the song slow down over time, and you can have multiple changes throughout your song.

Reverb, distortion, glitches, and delay

Effects such as reverb, distortion, glitches, and delay are tools available to create unnatural sounds. Usually, the goal is to have just enough reverb and delay to support existing sounds without drawing attention to the effect, but this is not the case if you're trying to create strange out-of-this-world sounds. Go crazy and crank up the reverb, delay, distortion, or any other effects you can think of.

We've discussed techniques and effects to create creepy music. We're missing one important element though – what notes to use with our instruments to create creepy and scary music. Let's learn this next.

Creepy and scary music note combinations

Certain note combinations sound familiar and soothing, but others can sound very unfamiliar and unsettling. In this section, we'll discuss note combinations that can be used to create creepy or scary music. The techniques we'll discuss include the following:

- The build-up of a creepy high-pitched sound paired with a creepy low-pitched sound
- Notes in a minor key
- Clashing notes
- Wrong notes
- Incrementing notes by fixed ratios

The build-up of a creepy high-pitched sound combined with a creepy low-pitched sound

One situation that is unnatural and often considered creepy is the pairing of a high sound simultaneously with a low sound, with relatively few middle frequencies. This is uncommon in nature. Usually, a sound source creates noise encompassing low frequencies, high frequencies, or the whole spectrum. But rarely do you hear just the low and the high frequencies coming from a singular sound source with nothing in the middle.

This rare sound can make your ears listen up and pay attention, as they're hearing something they don't normally expect. To create this effect, layer an instrument with a predominantly low frequency with an instrument that has a predominantly high frequency.

Notes in a minor key

Notes in a minor key have the impression of either being sad or scary. If played with soft-sounding instruments, they come across as sad or beautiful. If played with creepy-sounding instruments, they come across as spooky.

Clashing notes

If you want to create a jump scare and need a sound that will jump out at the listener and grab their attention, you may want to consider using clashing notes. Clashing notes are notes that are very dissonant.

Specifically, note combinations that clash include the following:

- A root note and a note three whole tones away played simultaneously. An example is shown in the following screenshot:

Figure 6.13 – Three whole tones apart

In the preceding screenshot, I've chosen a note combination that is three whole tones apart – in this case, C and F#. You can use any notes as long as they maintain a distance of three whole tones.

- Any two notes a semitone apart played simultaneously, as shown in the following screenshot:

Figure 6.14 – A semitone apart

In the preceding screenshot, you can see the two notes, C and B, a semitone apart. These note examples aren't restricted to being directly next to each other and can be spread out across octaves.

Wrong notes

In most music, we expect songs to stick within a given key. Notes within a key harmonize well together. This is pleasant to listen to. If you want to take the opposite approach, you can create music that is unpleasant to listen to. Play wrong notes that don't belong in the given key, or you could even consider starting with notes in one key and then drift out of that key into a jumbled mess.

If you're looking to generate chaotic, random notes, the FL Studio Piano roll has a tool called **Randomize**, designed precisely for creating random note variations.

The following steps show how to generate random notes instantly:

1. Choose a pattern and open up the Piano roll.
2. Select the **Tools | Randomize** option, as shown in the following screenshot:

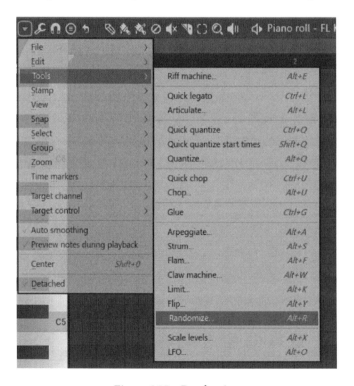

Figure 6.15 – Randomize

3. The **Randomize** tool will appear. Select the **Seed** button, as shown in the following screenshot:

Figure 6.16 – A random pattern

Notes will be randomly generated in the Piano roll for the selected pattern. The following describes the controls of the randomizer:

- **Octave**: Chooses what octave to begin generating random notes

- **Range**: Chooses how many octaves the random notes will span

- **Key / scale**: Confines the notes to a given key

- **Snapping to chord**: Restricts notes to a given chord

- **Length**: Chooses how long you want the notes to sustain for

- **Variation**: Chooses how much variation you want in the note lengths

- **Population**: Sets how many notes you want to generate

- **Stack**: Chooses how many notes you want to allow to be stacked upon each other

- **Random portamento**: Allows randomness to be generated for portamento articulations (sliding notes that often occur in string instruments)

- **Glue same notes**: Merges two notes if they are touching

- **Seed**: Generates new random note combinations

After playing with the randomizer settings and choosing **Accept**, you'll see that random notes are generated, as shown in the following screenshot:

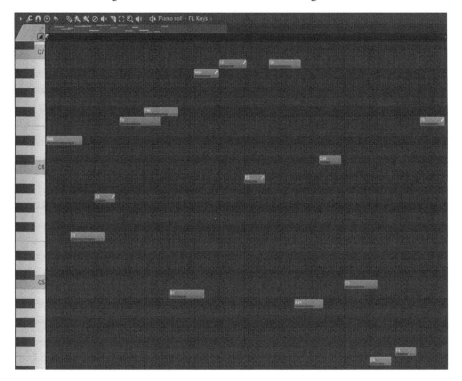

Figure 6.17 – Random notes

If you don't like the current version of your notes, you can always continue pressing the randomizer's **Seed** button to generate new random variations.

Incrementing by fixed ratios

If you like the idea of creating irregular note combinations that sound chaotic, there are multiple ways to achieve this. Usually, inserting randomness will achieve the effect you want. But what if we don't want the complete chaos that comes from hitting random notes in our sound? Is there a repeatable method for creating more coherent notes that still sound *off*? Yes, there is.

Most scales are confined to notes within a single octave. The restriction of notes gives the song structure and makes the melodies predictable to the listener.

If you want something that just sounds unusual and out of the ordinary, you can consider incrementing by constant intervals. For example, the whole tone scale uses notes that increment by whole tones. The following three screenshots show examples of how you can increment by fixed interval ratios:

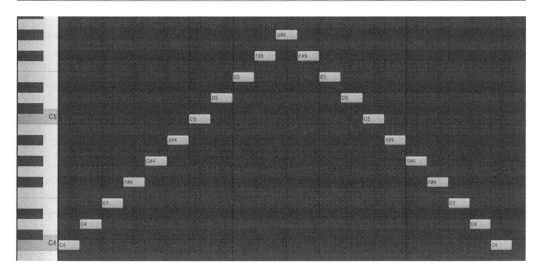

Figure 6.18 – Incrementing by whole tones

The preceding screenshot shows increments by two semitones, also known as a **whole tone**.

You can pick different fixed intervals in many ways. The following screenshot shows what you get if you increment by three semitones:

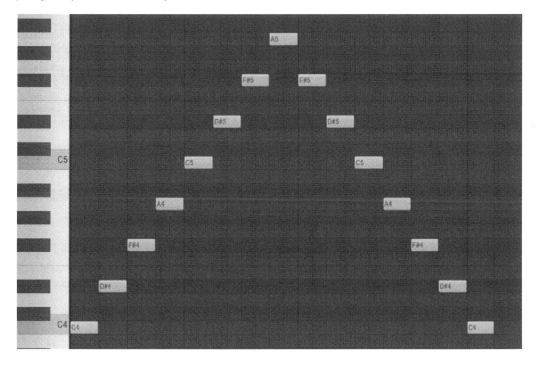

Figure 6.19 – Incrementing by three semitones

In all these examples, I'm using C as the root note, but you could use any note as your root. The following screenshot shows what happens if you increment by four semitones:

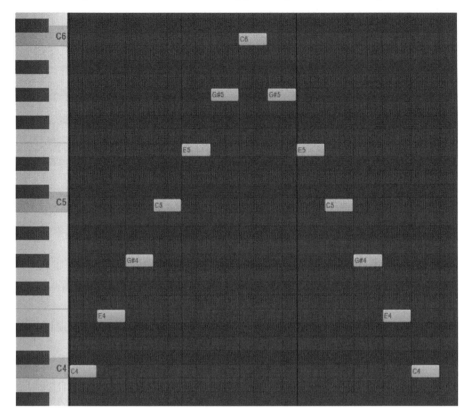

Figure 6.20 – Incrementing by four semitones

Using note combinations incremented by fixed ratios generates a very strange sound. If played on the right instrument, it can come across as quite creepy indeed.

So far, we've learned how to create music to scare an audience and how to design a jump scare. It's composed of a creepy build-up of music, followed by a brief quieting down for a moment of anticipation, and then a big reveal with a scary sound to shock the audience.

We learned about sounds that can be used to shock listeners, techniques and effects that can be used to create creepy sounds, and note combinations that can be used for creating scary or creepy music. When composing scary music, we looked at sounds that are dissonant – that is, they clash and disagree with each other and are unexpected and unfamiliar.

Now, let's venture into more familiar musical territory and learn how to create music for specific moods.

Composing music for specific moods

Some scenes in films require specific moods. As a film composer, you'd likely be given some direction about the type of mood a scene calls for. It's then your job to go and figure out how to compose music for that mood.

The techniques in this section are intended to serve as general guidelines for composing music for specific moods. They are not hard and fast rules though; there's lots of room to experiment. But if you need a place to start, these guidelines should help you get the ball rolling.

There are lots of techniques to create music for a given mood. You may want to start by researching how songs were made for similar moods in other projects, or you may want to check out various scales to see whether there's one that delivers a sound close to the mood you're aiming for.

If you want to check out some scales, you can check out the website `https://femurdesign.com/omni/`, which allows you to quickly explore how a variety of scales sound. The following screenshot shows the OMNI tool found on the website:

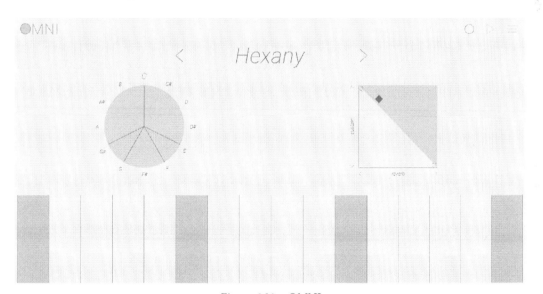

Figure 6.21 – OMNI

OMNI allows you to quickly navigate through scales and see how notes sound in a given key. At the top is the chosen scale, which you can navigate through. On the left-hand side, you'll find a chord wheel, allowing you to choose a root note for the scale. On the right is a controller that lets you control how much reverb and sustain a sound effect has. At the bottom, you'll find a keyboard, allowing you to play notes in the scale.

This website is handy if you want to quickly browse through some scales and hear what they sound like.

Composing happy music

Happy music makes up most of the music you hear on the radio. If you look at the hit songs on the charts, the majority of them are in major sounding modes. Why? Major modes are recognized by the listener as happy sounding music. Happy music makes people feel happy, and people like feeling happy. In this section, we'll take a look at tips for composing happy music.

> If you're wondering why major modes sound happy, check out the following video by Adam Neely:
>
> ```
> https://www.youtube.com/watch?v=9rEqrPwVITY&ab_
> channel=AdamNeely
> ```

The following techniques should be considered when composing music for a happy mood:

- **Major modes – Ionian, Lydian, and Mixolydian**: The most important factor in whether a song sounds happy or not is the note choice. There are three modes that work well for composing happy-sounding music. These are the **Ionian**, **Lydian**, and **Mixolydian** modes. If you're looking for a shortcut approach for composing happy music, pick notes that fit into these scales. If you need a refresher, we discussed modes in detail in *Chapter 3, Designing Music with Themes, Leitmotifs, and Scales*.

- **A lively tempo – not necessarily fast but lively**: Happy music often has a lively tempo. If you play music while walking from one place to another, you may notice that your pace tends to be in tempo with the song you're listening to. This is not a coincidence. Your body instinctively reacts to its surroundings. Slow music makes you want to slow down, and fast music makes you want to speed up.

  When doing a brisk walk, the human heart beats around 110–120 beats per minute. If you want your listener to be moving at a walking speed, aim for this range. If you want your listener to be moving faster, you can increase the tempo. Most electronic dance music tends to have tempos in the range of 124–130 bpm. It's a good speed for a jog, dance, or run if you pace your steps to the beat of the song.

- **Favor hard sounds over soft sounds**: Punchy sounds deliver more energy than softer sounds with a slower attack. Drums and percussive instruments are generally harder, punchier sounds. So, if you are lacking energy in your songs, consider inserting some drums or more percussive sounds.

- **Consonant sounds**: Happy music relies on notes that harmonize well with each other. If you want happy music, favor note combinations that are consonant. Lean away from dissonant sounds. That's not to say that you should avoid using notes in a scale just because they're initially dissonant; just find ways to make them more in harmony with each other. For example, if you were planning on using a root note with a 7th note, which is initially quite dissonant, consider making the chord into a dominant 7th chord. This is more harmonious sounding. You're still using a seventh note; you've just added some notes to make the chord harmonize more.

- **Rhythms**: Rhythm can transform a flat chord progression into a catchy melody that sticks in your head. Your ears find multiple rhythms much more interesting than a single rhythm. Each instrument playing notes can have its own rhythm. You can have multiple rhythms playing simultaneously across different instruments. For example, the drums are playing one rhythm, the piano chords are playing another, and the bass guitar is playing a third. If chosen carefully, the instruments can feel like they're playing off each other.

- **Upward motion**: Note progression that moves upward in pitch is perceived as increasing in energy. If you want to create the impression of uplifting music, lean toward upward note and chord progressions.

We've now learned how to create happy music. Next, let's look at the opposite and learn how to compose sad music.

Composing sad music

As you would expect, composing sad music is, in many ways, the opposite of composing happy music. Most of the techniques you would use to make happy music can be inverted to make sad music.

The following techniques can be used to make sad sounding music:

- **Minor modes – Aeolian, Phrygian, Dorian, and Locrian**: The quickest way to make a song sound sad is to use minor note choices. The modes that are recognized as sadder sounding include Aeolian, Phrygian, Dorian, and Locrian.

  If you need a refresher, we discussed modes in detail in *Chapter 3, Designing Music with Themes, Leitmotifs, and Scales*.

  Certain note combination choices can also make your music sound sad. If you're wondering what notes to add in your next chord progression, consider adding suspended chords, including suspended 2nds, 4ths, 7ths, and 9ths.

> **Note**
>
> If you want some detailed music theory tutorials to get a stronger grasp on suspended chords, consider visiting this YouTube channel by Michael New: `https://www.youtube.com/c/MichaelNew/featured`. It contains lots of in-depth explanations about chord theory and what makes up suspended chords.

- **Slow tempo**: Sad music is usually accompanied by a slower tempo. Remember that the average heartbeat of a person when taking a brisk walk is around 110–120 beats per minute. If you want sadder music, you should probably aim for a tempo slower than a brisk walk.

  Tempo can affect a piece of music, even if it is in a minor key. The theme song for the *Pirates of the Caribbean* movies, composed by Hans Zimmer, is one example. Zimmer wondered what would happen if he wrote the song in a minor key and increased the tempo to make it fast. The result is a much more energetic-sounding song that is now the theme song for the movie franchise. The *Pirates of the Caribbean* theme doesn't sound sad, even though it's in a minor key. The fast tempo and 6/8 time signature create an entirely new feel. If you want to create a unique style, consider how changing the speed or time signature could affect the feel of your music.

- **Lots of space between notes**: With fast songs, you can cram in lots of notes, as they'll be played quickly. With sadder slower songs, you want to milk your notes for longer. Draw them out.

- **Allow notes to ring out**: In slow, sad songs, you can make the most of atmospheric sounds. This is a great place for long droning sounds, with drawn-out pads, strings, and sustained piano notes.

- **Reverb**: If you want your sounds to be lengthy and drawn out, reverb should be the first thing that comes to mind. Reverb is an effect that simulates the sound of echoes in a space and allows your sounds to ring out longer.

- **Give each instrument space**: In dance songs, you quickly alternate from one instrument to the next. You're depending on rhythms to play off one another. In sad songs, you don't need to cram in a bunch of instruments simultaneously. You can give your instruments space when going from one to the next. You also have the opportunity to play around with solo instruments and let them shine.

- **Vibrato to add extra emotion**: Long drawn-out notes can be made more expressive through the use of vibrato. If you're using string instruments, vibrato is a useful articulation whenever you want to add emotional emphasis.

- **Legato articulations**: With fast music, you rely on punctuated sounds with percussive instruments. With sad music, you want your sounds to blur into one another. Legato articulations allow you to create this sound.

- **Soft sounding instruments**: If you want notes to blur into one another, you'll want to think about using instruments that naturally blend together. In sad music, you want soft-sounding instruments. String instruments, such as the violin or cello, are excellent choices for this.

- **Downward motion**: Upward note progressions are connected with uplifting and happier melodies. Downward note progression, usually a descending bassline, is associated with sadder melodies.

We've learned about techniques for composing sad-sounding music. Next, let's learn how to compose romantic music.

Composing romantic music

Romantic music is the combination of happy and sad music. It's walking the middle line between them, combining both emotions without going too far in either direction. The sad elements make the listener feel reflective and heavy, while the happy elements make the listener feel joyful and light.

The following techniques can be used to create romantic music.

- **Minor modes – Aeolian, Phrygian, Dorian, Locrian**: Minor modes can be associated with sadness, but they can also be associated with beauty. Most romantic music is composed in minor modes.

- **String instruments and soft percussive instruments**: String instruments have the ability to be extremely expressive. They allow you to use vibrato articulations on drawn-out notes. Cellos and violins are often associated with romantic music. Violins can give the impression of soaring melodies above the rest of the orchestra, which works well in many romantic pieces. Soft percussive instruments, such as harps and pianos, are also ideal for romantic sounds. In general, you'll want to avoid hard, punchy, percussive sounds.

- **Legato and vibrato**: Generally, you should favor long-drawn-out expressive notes that blend into one another. Legato articulations allow you to blend notes into one another seamlessly. You can make long drawn-out notes more expressive using vibrato.

- **Slow tempo**: Romantic pieces usually involve slower tempos.

We've learned how to create romantic music. Next, let's learn how to create tension.

Creating tension/composing epic music for trailers

So far, we've focused on specific moods: happy, sad, and romantic. What if you need your song to have lots of energy and tension? If you're composing trailers for films, you'll sometimes be required to compose what is known as **epic music**. This is often needed for trailers. Epic music is music that feels powerful and intense.

Here are a few techniques to create the feeling of tension in your scenes:

- **Big drums**: If you want your music to feel big and powerful, a quick way is to introduce the sound of large drums, such as kettle drums, bass drums, gongs, timpani, and large cymbals. Create percussive rhythms and layer drum sounds on top of one another.

  Adding the effects of compression and reverb can make your drums sound larger. Reverb is a fancy term for simulating echoes. The larger the space an object is in, the more sound reflections are possible, and the larger the instrument and the environment, the more opportunity for echoes.

- **Bass and brass instruments**: Large, deep sounds convey size and depth. If you want to make something feel more epic, you'll want to have a strong bass instrument underlying the score.

  The orchestral brass section has the ability to convey powerful sounds, so you may want to consider including instruments from this section. Horns tend to cut right through the mix and stand out. Brass family instruments include the trumpet, the French horn, the trombone, and the tuba.

- **Low deep sounds**: If you want to convey the size and scale of a large scene, you want to have deep low sounds. To create this, seek out instruments that are large or simulate them. Large instruments also create large reverberations, so you'll want to find a reverb that supports the sound.

- **Shepard tone**: In the film *Dunkirk*, which was nominated for an Academy Award for its music, composer Hans Zimmer used a technique known as a Shepard tone in the creation of much of its score. A Shepard tone is the term used to describe a rising pitch that seems like it never ends. It keeps building and building forever.

The following screenshot shows an example of a Shepard tone waveform:

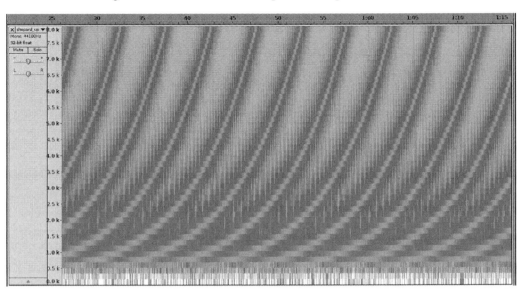

Figure 6.22 – A Shepard tone

https://upload.wikimedia.org/wikipedia/commons/4/48/Shepard_Tones_spectrum_linear_scale.png

Creating a Shepard tone is not as simple as increasing the frequency of a sound. If you increase the frequency of a sound high enough, your ears will be unable to hear the sound anymore. Instead, what happens in a Shepard tone is that as the frequency of a sound approaches a high value, it begins to fade out. A new low frequency then fades in to replace the high one. This is done in a manner that makes it feel like it's continuously building.

If you want to know more about Shepard tones, you can watch the VOX video on the Shepard tone called *The sound illusion that makes Dunkirk so intense* (`https://youtu.be/LVWTQcZbLgY`).

- **Full harmonies**: Layer your sounds. If you're hitting a note, double up and/or hit the same note transposed across octaves with multiple instruments. Pay attention to the frequency low end. That's usually where the feeling of strength comes from. With layering, you can create powerful all-encompassing walls of sound.

- **Contrast**: Transition between moments of calm and intensity. Sounds will feel more intense if preceded by something that feels much calmer. The more intense scenes usually have more percussion and in-your-face bass sounds. So, you'll usually want to lead up to these moments of intensity over time rather than starting out with them.

- **Impacts**: The use of impact-sound samples can be used to great effect, such as explosions, or objects crashing, smashing, and breaking. Reversing these sounds is a great way to create anticipation.

- **Consider time signatures**: A lot of medieval and fantasy music uses a 6/8 time signature. This is commonly recognized as music that sounds like a march. Marching music has military connotations and can convey the idea of power and might. If this is what you're looking for, you may want to consider using a 6/8 time signature.

That concludes our learning about the techniques to create tension in your music.

Summary

In this chapter, we learned how to create music to evoke a range of emotions in our audience.

We learned the theory of creating fear with sound. We learned techniques to create scary and creepy music. We learned how these techniques can be used to design custom jump scares.

We learned how to create music for a variety of moods, from happy and sad to romantic. Finally, we learned how we can use music to create tension in a scene. Using the techniques in this chapter, we are able to design music for a variety of emotional scenarios.

In the next chapter, we'll learn how to create interactive music for video games.

7

Creating Interactive Music for Video Games with Wwise

This chapter will give you an introduction to creating interactive music for video games. You'll learn what interactive music is and the techniques of **horizontal re-sequencing** and **vertical remixing**.

We'll do this by using the **Wave Works Interactive Sound Engine** (**Wwise**) audio engine software, which allows you to customize how music is integrated into video games. In Wwise, we'll download a demo game that comes prebuilt with sounds and music. Using the demo game, we'll see how interactive music techniques can be applied. Finally, we'll learn how to create music in FL Studio for use in vertical remixing.

In this chapter, we'll cover the following topics:

- What is interactive music?
- Getting started with Wwise
- Understanding horizontal re-sequencing
- Implementing horizontal re-sequencing in Wwise
- Understanding vertical remixing

- Implementing vertical remixing in Wwise
- Creating music for vertical remixing in FL Studio

What is interactive music?

A video game requires a lot of music to be created. Anything that occurs in a game could require sound. Many of these sounds can change throughout the game. For each environment and level, you may want to consider creating music that adapts to the player's actions.

Here's a list of game sounds you might want to consider when composing for video games:

- Trailers
- Characters
- Button clicks
- Menus
- Loading level screens
- Entering new levels
- Completing levels
- Music for each boss
- Entering new rooms
- Obtaining items
- Achievements
- Ambient sounds for environments
- Battle sounds
- Cutscenes
- Music that characters are listening to within the game
- Victory
- Defeat

In order to create interactive music, you need tools to tell the game when to change the music. Some game-building software have tools for creating interactive music built in, and game engines are getting better tools every year. Currently, though, if you want fine control over everything, you'll likely want to learn a piece of middleware software designed specifically for creating interactive music.

There are several middleware software options on the market for creating interactive music. Two of the most popular are Wwise, available at `https://www.audiokinetic.com/`, and FMOD, available at `https://www.fmod.com/`. These two examples of software allow you to manipulate audio for video games and have integration support with game-developing software such as Unity and Unreal Engine (the two biggest game-developing software at the moment).

Both of these audio engine software offerings are great, and if you work on integrating sound for video games, it is very likely that you'll need to use Wwise or FMOD.

The following screenshot shows Wwise on the Audiokinetic website:

Figure 7.1 – Wwise by Audiokinetic

For the examples in this chapter, we will be using Wwise, so to follow along with the examples, you will need to download the software. You can download Wwise at `https://www.https://www.audiokinetic.com/`.

Getting started with Wwise

Let's install a demo game that comes with Wwise so we can see examples of how interactive music can be used.

Just a little heads up, the following steps are quite fiddly. Don't feel bad if you struggle a little to figure out how to use Wwise in the beginning. It is quite a complex software to wrap your head around the first time you encounter it:

1. After you download the installer from the Audiokinetic website, you'll be greeted with a window prompting you to download the latest version.

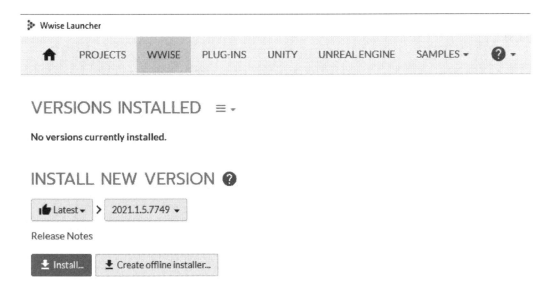

Figure 7.2 – Wwise Launcher

2. After selecting the **Install…** button, you'll encounter the following window:

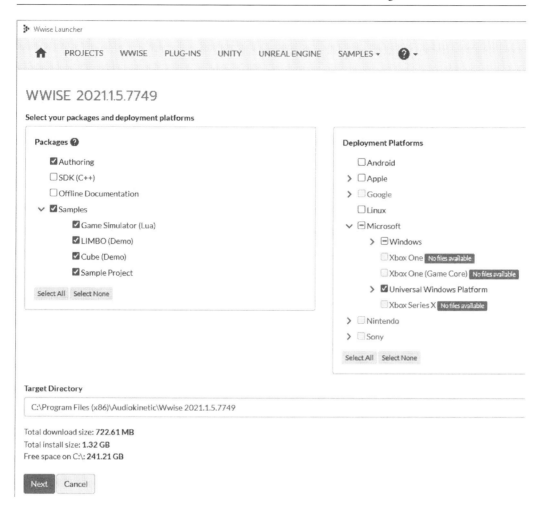

Figure 7.3 – Installing samples

3. Make sure you check **Samples** to get the demo files. Then, select the platform you want to deploy on.

    In this case, I'm using a Windows computer, so I've chosen **Windows**. Then, choose where on your computer you want to download the software.

4. In the preceding screenshot, I am downloading the Cube game as well as some other demo samples that I encourage you to check out. For the purposes of this chapter, we will be using the **Cube (Demo)** game, so make sure that you check this option.

5. Next, it will ask you whether you'd like to install any additional plugins. For our demo purposes, we won't add any extra plugins.

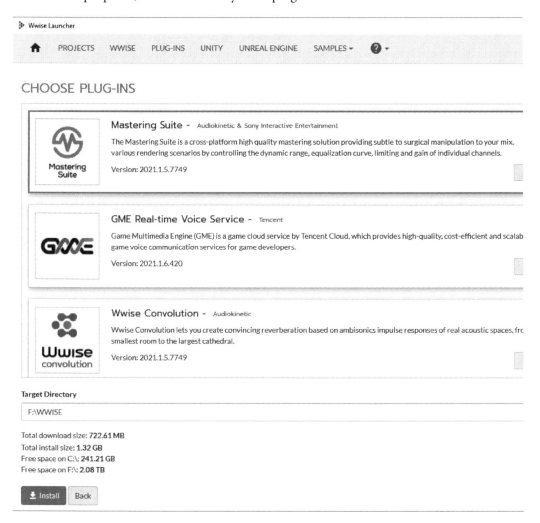

Figure 7.4 – Installing the Wwise software

6. Click **Install**. Wwise and the sample games will download.

7. After installing, in the Wwise Launcher, go to **SAMPLES | Wwise** and locate the Cube game, as shown in the following screenshot:

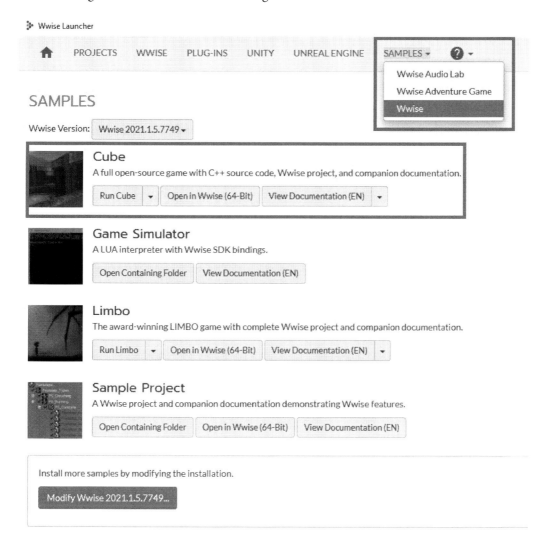

Figure 7.5 – Locating the Cube game

In the preceding screenshot, you can see there are several Wwise samples available. The one of importance to us is the Cube game.

8. I encourage you to play the Cube game by selecting the **Run Cube** option. This will load up a fully functional game. The following screenshot shows an example screen of the game:

Figure 7.6 – Cube gameplay

Take a few moments to experiment in Cube to get an idea of the gameplay. It's a first-person shooter-style game. You move around using the *W*, *A*, *S*, and *D* keys on your keyboard and use your mouse to look around and shoot.

9. If you press *Esc* on your keyboard, you can jump to different maps or quit the game, as shown by the following screenshot:

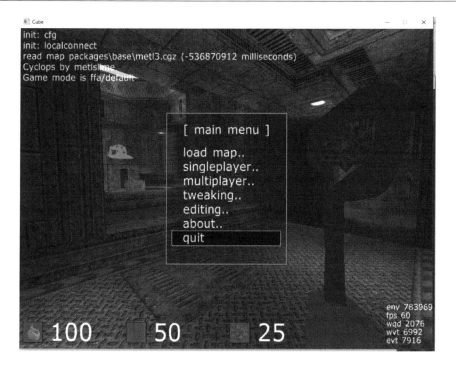

Figure 7.7 – Quitting Cube

We've got an idea of the game demo. Now it's time to look at how Wwise uses music inside the game:

1. Back in the Wwise Launcher, go to **SAMPLES** and select the **Open in Wwise (64-Bit)** option, as shown in the following screenshot:

Figure 7.8 – Opening Cube in Wwise

This will open the Cube game in Wwise.

2.   When you first open Wwise, you should see the designer layout. If not, press *F5* and the workstation will open it up, as shown in the following screenshot:

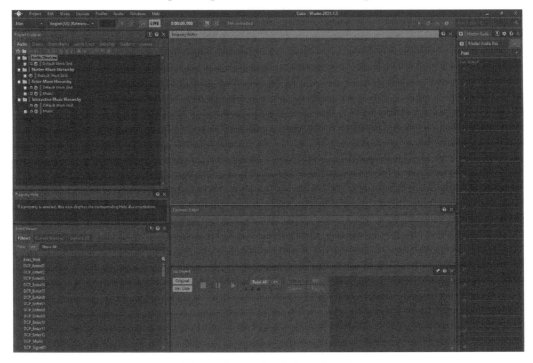

Figure 7.9 – Wwise designer layout

On the left-hand side, you'll see a workstation with **Project Explorer**.

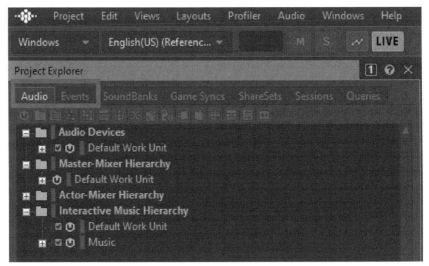

Figure 7.10 – Project Explorer

We opened up the Cube demo game in Wwise. You'll find it has been populated with sounds for the demo, so there's a lot of stuff already set up for us to see.

If you look under **Project Explorer**, you'll see the **Audio** and **Events** tabs. **Audio** contains all of the audio samples you've loaded in the game. **Events** lists the events to trigger audio samples to play.

In the preceding screenshot, we can see the **Audio** tab is currently selected. There are folders of audio where sound samples can be loaded and played. If you expand the folders and explore a bit, you'll find tons of sounds that are currently being used in the game, as shown in the following screenshot:

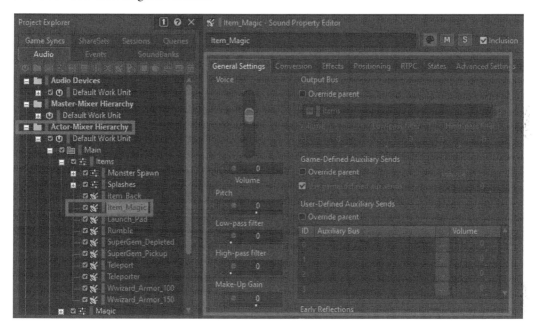

Figure 7.11 – Playing a sound

You can listen to any of the sounds by left-clicking to select it and then pressing the spacebar. Selecting an audio sample will open up the Sound Property Editor, where you can make adjustments to the sound, such as changing the pitch or adding filters and effects.

The **Events** tab lists the event triggers to signal when the game should perform an action, such as playing a specific audio file. The following screenshot shows the **Events** tab:

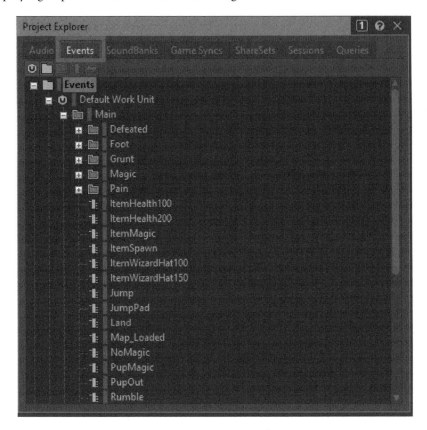

Figure 7.12 – Events tab

When an event is triggered in the game, you tell it to play a sound that was loaded in the **Audio** tab folders. Events are originally created in the game-designing engine. In other words, events are created in Unreal Engine, Unity, or whatever game engine you happen to be using. In the game engine, you would designate an event to be linked to Wwise. The steps to do this are game engine-specific, so the topic goes beyond the scope of this chapter. Fortunately, for our example, the Cube game already has events created for our use.

In the following screenshot, we can see that the **ItemHealth100** event is told to play the **Item_Magic** and **Health_Cue** audio, which are files that exist in the **Audio** tab folders:

Figure 7.13 – Event triggering audio to play

For every event trigger in the game, you can designate an audio sample for the event to play. On the right, you can also assign a probability of playing the audio file so that it only plays audio sometimes, so it doesn't get too repetitive.

Creating new sounds for a game involves you knowing the event names. So, you need to have a list of the exact name spellings of the events that you want to trigger.

The events are created in the game itself and you use the same name in Wwise, so if you were working on an actual game, you'd need to coordinate with the developers to figure out what event names should be used.

We've learned the basics of how sounds and events work in Wwise. Wwise is a huge topic that would require a book in itself to learn fully. The goal of this chapter is to focus on learning about interactive music, rather than learning everything about Wwise. So, let's dive into our first interactive music topic: horizontal re-sequencing.

Understanding horizontal re-sequencing

Horizontal re-sequencing allows you to shift between music tracks seamlessly, combining several song tracks to feel like a single song.

Without horizontal re-sequencing, you'd play one music track, then wait until it's over before playing the next piece. This can sound abrupt and take the player out of the moment when they're playing the game. If you want a natural and immersive experience, you usually want music to feel like it's flowing from one song to the next without sudden breaks.

Also, if you play the exact same song over and over, it can come across as very repetitive and bore the listener. Horizontal re-sequencing allows you to flip between audio samples and add random variation in choosing which song track to play next.

Horizontal re-sequencing helps shift between song clips. If it's done correctly, the listener won't realize they listened to several different clips. It will feel like one cohesive song with variation that can keep looping indefinitely.

Implementing horizontal re-sequencing in Wwise

The Cube demo has an example of horizontal re-sequencing built in. Let's take a moment to see how the Cube game uses horizontal re-sequencing:

1. Go to the **Interactive Music** layout, as shown in the following screenshot. You can also press *F10* to access this layout:

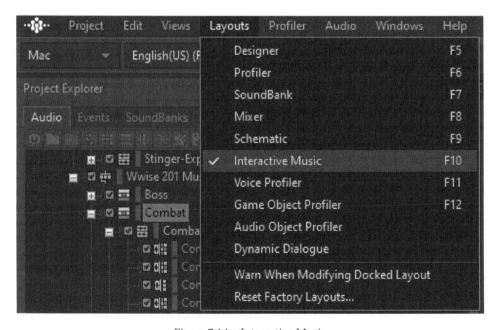

Figure 7.14 – Interactive Music

2. Under **Interactive Music Hierarchy**, select the **Combat** folder.

3. After selecting the **Combat** folder, press the spacebar and you'll hear music begin to play. Notice a little yellow arrow appearing beside the track currently playing in **Music Playlist Editor**. As the music plays, it will shift from one track to the next, as shown in the following screenshot:

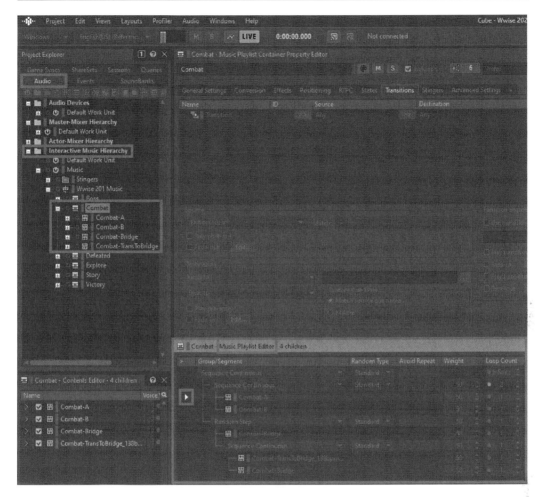

Figure 7.15 – Horizontal re-sequencing

The music plays **Combat-A** and **Combat-B** sequentially. Then, there's a 50% probability it will play **Combat-Bridge**, and then a 50% probability that it plays the **Combat-TransToBridge** and **Combat-Bridge** tracks.

The game is playing a loop, but a loop that varies according to set probabilities. Sometimes it plays just the **Combat-A** and **Combat-B** tracks. Sometimes it plays **Combat-Bridge**, and sometimes it plays the **Combat-TransToBridge** and **Combat-Bridge** tracks. Playing music in this manner helps to create some random variation in audio for the listener.

Music segments can be dragged from the **Audio** tab into **Music Playlist Editor**. You can then designate the order and the probability of the song playing that you want.

You may be wondering what some of the terms that appear in **Music Playlist Editor** mean:

- **Weight** means the probability of playing the track. You can assign probabilities to randomize whether a track plays next in the sequence or not.

- **Loop Count** means how many times the sequence group play should be repeated before moving on.

- **Sequence Continuous** means that it will play all tracks in the sequence group one after another.

- **New Group** allows you to add a condition of when you want the containing music segment to play. You have the option between sequential (playing in order) or adding some randomness as to when the track should be played according to the weight you assign. The following screenshot shows an example.

- **Random Step** allows you to randomly choose between options. In the following screenshot, it means it might flip to the **Combat-Bridge** or the **Combat-TransToBridge** track:

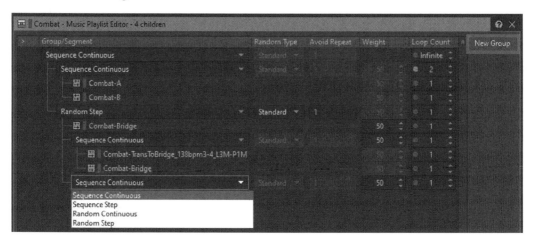

Figure 7.16 – Music Playlist Editor showing horizontal re-sequencing

Any time you have looping in a video game, it's an opportunity to create music that changes over time using horizontal re-sequencing to create some music variability for the listener. Used correctly, your music will feel less repetitive.

We've seen an example of how horizontal re-sequencing is done in Wwise. Next, let's learn about vertical remixing.

Understanding vertical remixing

Depending on what event is happening in any given level, you can turn on or off layers of a song. This is very similar to how you can layer instruments and turn layers on and off in FL Studio.

Vertical remixing is the term describing how you can mix in different audio layers during the game runtime. In vertical remixing, you have a series of audio clips in a song that you choose to play or not depending on a condition set in the game.

For example, as you enter a level, a song begins to play with a simple melody. As you encounter an enemy, new melodies and instruments layer on top of the original melody. It's the same song, but you've just turned on additional layers of music.

Implementing vertical remixing in Wwise

You can do vertical remixing through several techniques. Wwise allows you to use states, switches, real-time parameter controls, and triggers. These are all controls that you can use in Wwise. Any of these methods can be used to turn audio on or off.

All you need are certain conditions to be met so you can enable layers of your song to be turned on or off. You'll also want to gracefully transition between turning audio layers on and off so the sound changes gradually, rather than abruptly.

In the following example, we'll continue using the Cube demo project. We'll create a new switch, then tell our music to turn on or off depending on the value of a switch. Finally, we'll learn how to gracefully transition music layers on and off by fading layers in and out.

Let's learn how to implement vertical remixing in Wwise:

1. First, make sure you're in the **Interactive Music** layout, as shown in the following screenshot. You can also press *F10* to access this layout. If you find you're missing some panels throughout the example, check that you are in the **Interactive Music** layout as leaving this could cause panels to not appear onscreen:

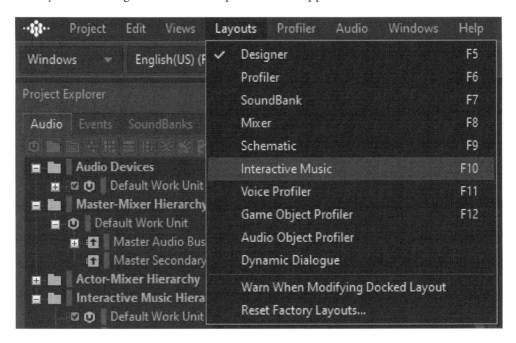

Figure 7.17 – Interactive Music layout

2. We need to create a switch. In the **Game Syncs** tab, right-click on **Music** and create a new switch group, as shown in the following screenshot:

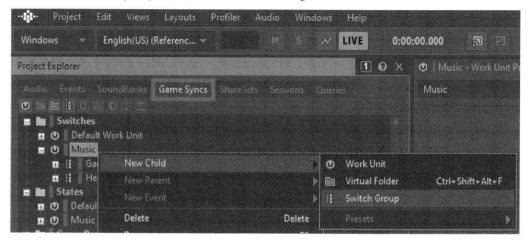

Figure 7.18 – Creating a switch group

3. Give it a name; in my case, I've called it Energy_Level. Right-click on the switch group, then create at least two new switches and give them names. In my case, I'll call them High_Energy and Low_Energy. The following screenshot shows an example of creating a switch:

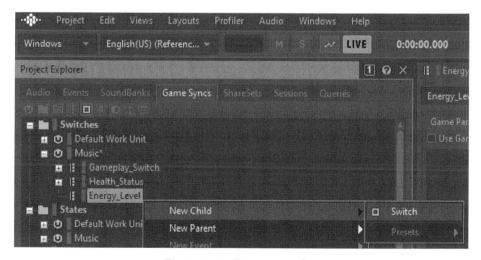

Figure 7.19 – Creating switches

You've created a switch group and added switches inside it. Now we need to connect our music segment to the switches.

4. In the **Audio** tab, locate a music segment. In my example using the Cube demo game, I've chosen a segment of pre-existing guitar instruments, as shown in the following screenshot:

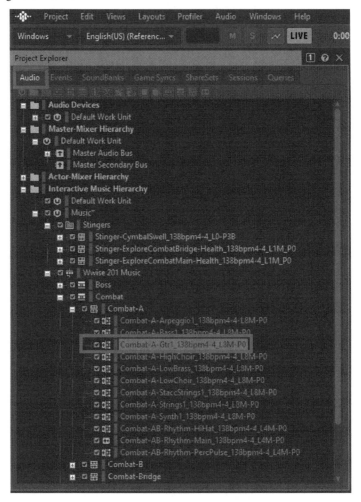

Figure 7.20 – Selecting a guitar segment

5. Double-left-click on the music segment. In the preceding screenshot, I selected **Combat-A-Gtr1_138bpm4-4_L8M-P0**. This will open up **Music Track Property Editor**.

6. In **Music Track Property Editor**, navigate to the **General Settings** tab. Set **Track Type** to **Switch**, **Group** to the switch container name, which in my case is **Energy_ Level**, and the default switch state, which in my case is **Low_Energy**. These are the names of switches that you have just created. The following screenshot shows an example:

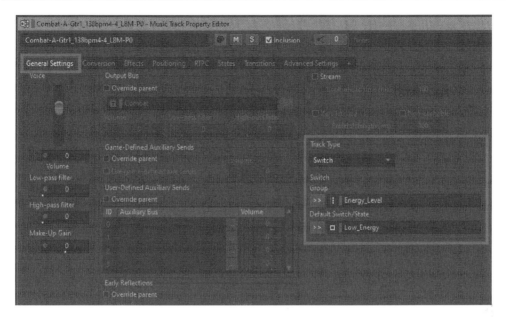

Figure 7.21 – Setting Track Type, Group, and Default Switch/State

We've enabled our segment to be able to use switches. Now we need to tell Wwise what audio to play depending on the switch value.

7. In **Music Segment Editor**, right-click on the button next to the audio track you want to connect to the switch, select **Set Association**, and choose the switch value you want to use to play the audio, as shown in the following screenshot:

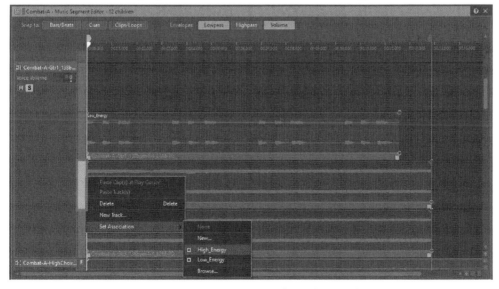

Figure 7.22 – Connecting audio with a switch

8.   Repeat *step 7* for each audio clip you want to connect to a switch.

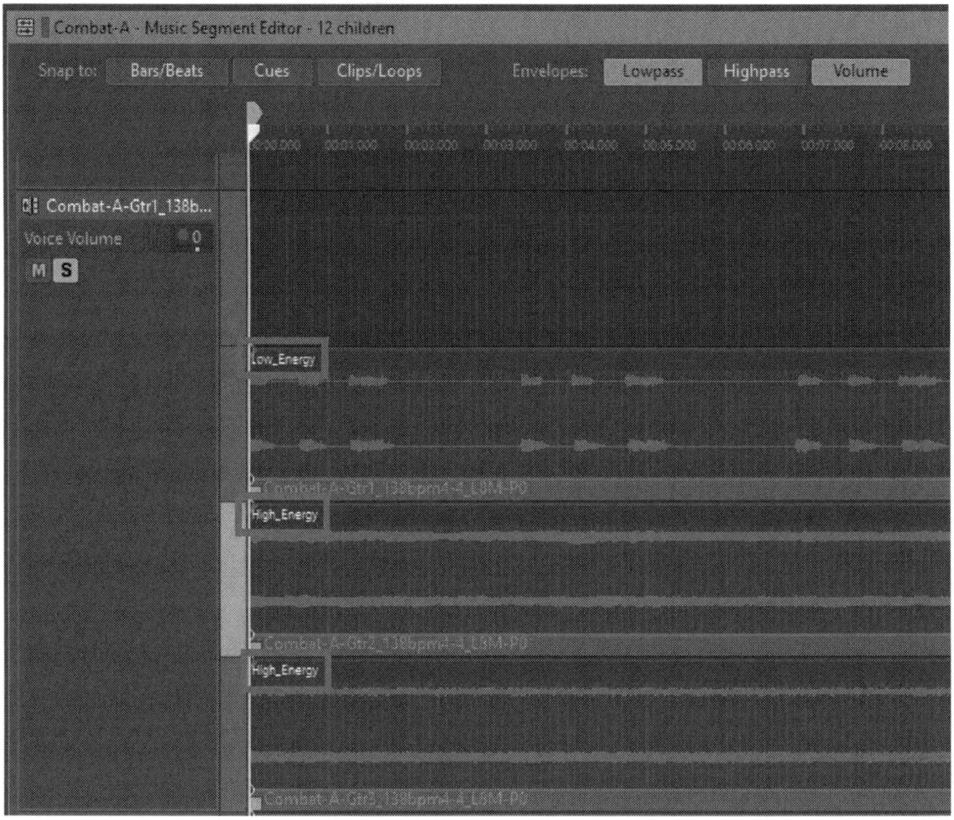

Figure 7.23 – Audio

After you've connected the audio clip with the switch, you should see the name of the switch label appear on the audio clip, as shown in the preceding screenshot.

9.   Let's test whether our switch is working. *Solo* the audio clips by left-clicking on the **S** button in **Music Segment Editor** for clips you want to listen to. Press the spacebar. You'll hear the music segment play with audio that is assigned to the default switch value.

10. Let's use our switch and hear how the audio changes. In the **Transport Control** panel, navigate to the **Switches** tab. You'll see the switch container and switches you just created. In my case, the switch container name is **Energy_Level** and the default switch state is set to **Low_Energy**.

11. As you press the spacebar to listen to the music segment, left-click on the drop-down box as shown in the following screenshot and flip between the switch values, as shown in the following screenshot:

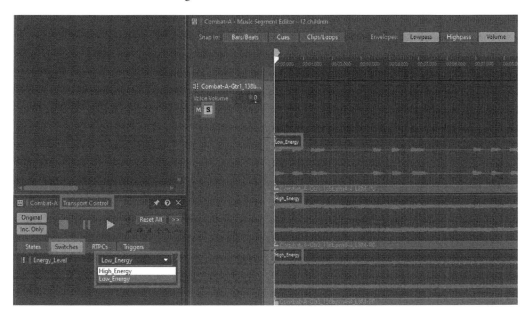

Figure 7.24 – Transport Control

The music segment is playing audio clips depending on the switch values. If the switch is set to **Low_Energy**, the audio clips connected to **Low_Energy** will play.

Congratulations, we have our music playing with vertical remixing! Depending on the switch state, different layers of audio will now turn on or off. This can be done anytime you want music to change depending on game activities.

The music currently changes abruptly whenever you change the switch value. It would sound better if the music gradually faded in and out. Let's learn how to do this.

1. In **Music Track Property Editor**, select the **Transitions** tab.

2. Select the item called **Transition** in the list.

3. Set **Exit source** at to the **Next Bar** value.

4. Make sure that **Fade-out** and **Fade-in** are checked. If you want to edit how long it takes to fade in or out, you can select the **Edit…** button next to the **Fade-out** and **Fade-in** buttons and adjust the time.

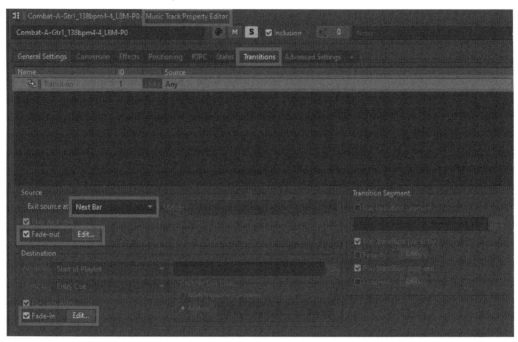

Figure 7.25 – Music Track Property Editor transitions

If you play your music segment and change the switch value in the **Transport Control** panel, you will hear clips gradually turning on and off, fading in and out.

Our music now gracefully transitions between layers of music. You now know how to use Wwise to create music for vertical remixing.

> **Note**
>
> If you want more examples, the *Unlock Audio* YouTube channel provides some great Wwise tutorials: `https://www.youtube.com/watch?v=mivXVv3QBaE&ab_channel=UnlockAudio`.
>
> If you'd like to see videos that go into Wwise in more depth, Audiokinetic offers tutorials on their products on their YouTube channel: `https://www.youtube.com/channel/UCuv_-Z-CrnYup-N_dVpdCYg`.

We've learned how to integrate music for vertical remixing in Wwise. However, you may be wondering how we get music layers that are perfectly in sync with one another. Is there an easy way to export layers in a song for use in vertical remixing? Yes, there is.

Let's learn how to create music for vertical remixing in FL Studio next.

Creating music for vertical remixing in FL Studio

There are a few steps needed to prepare music for vertical remixing. Vertical remixing is where you have layers of song clips that can be turned on and off. We need several instrumental layers that are in sync and sound good together.

The way we do this is to take an existing song in FL Studio and organize parts of the song as layers. These layers are then exported.

We need to create a series of layers that piece together to make one song, and then export the layers as separate files. These layers are then recombined and stacked on top of each other back in Wwise.

Each layer of music used in vertical remixing should sound good and be in sync with other layers in the song. At a minimum, this means the layers should be in the same key and be at the same tempo. What you include in any given layer is up to you, but you will want to plan this out ahead of time.

The following screenshot shows a simplistic example of a song with layers for vertical remixing created in FL Studio:

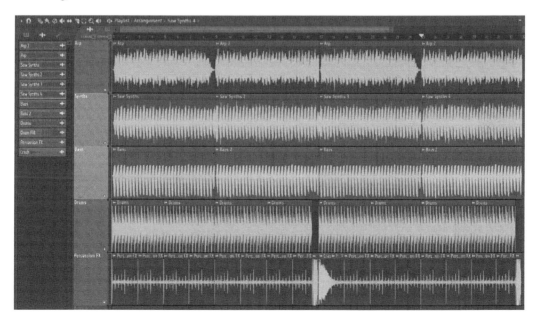

Figure 7.26 – Layers in FL Studio

In the preceding screenshot, you can see I've created five layers. There's an arpeggiating instrument layer, a synth layer, a bass layer, a drums layer, and a percussion FX layer. I've routed all the sounds in these layers to their own mixer channel tracks, as shown in the following screenshot:

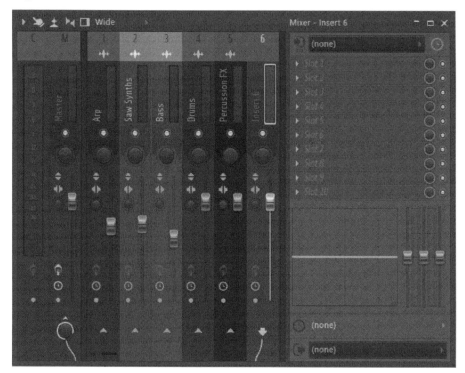

Figure 7.27 – Routing each layer to its own mixer track

In the preceding screenshot, we can see the five mixer channel tracks: **Arp**, **Saw Synths**, **Bass**, **Drums**, and **Percussion FX**. These have been carefully labeled. Later, when we export the song, it will use the names of these channel tracks, so it's important that we can identify what the tracks are by name.

When we export the song, we can export each of these mixer channels as their own audio clip. This will export the song layer clips in sync with the same length and time as all the other layers. This is important for when we want to recombine them later on.

Let's learn how to export a song ready for vertical remixing:

1. Make sure you've properly routed your tracks to mixer channels and labeled the channels so you can identify song layers later on.

2. When ready to export your song, go to **FILE | Export | Wave file…**, as shown in the following screenshot:

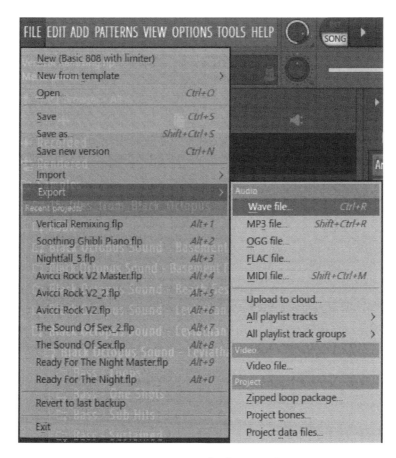

Figure 7.28 – Exporting audio for vertical remixing

After choosing a location of where to save the file, you will see the rendering window pop up, as shown in the following screenshot:

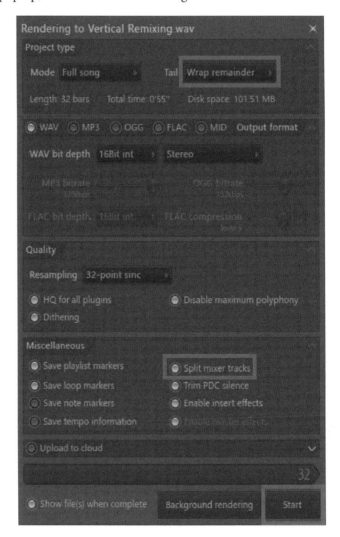

Figure 7.29 – Exporting audio for Vertical Remixing

3. If you want your clips to be loopable, make sure that **Wrap remainder** is selected. Normally, when your song plays, if you have any reverb effects, this will play after the song has completed and will gradually be faded out. If you're only playing a song once, this is usually what you want. However, if you want song clips to loop, then you want reverb from the end of the loop to play when the loop begins a second time. This way, you won't notice an abrupt transition between clips. Selecting **Wrap remainder** allows this to happen.

If instead of choosing **Wrap remainder** you choose the **Cut Remainder** option, you will hear the song fade out gradually and any fading reverb. This may be desirable if you don't want the song to abruptly end once the song finishes. It just depends on whether you want to hear the reverb when the loop plays again.

Also, it's important to note that the first time you hear a song clip play, you might not want to hear the ending reverb loop at the start. It's a case-by-case sort of situation you'll need to consider. You might want to export two versions, one with **Wrap remainder** and one with **Cut Remainder**, so you have access to both versions.

4. Make sure that **Split mixer tracks** is turned on. This will make a new track out of each mixer track channel. This option is only available if you are exporting WAV files. If you don't see this option available, make sure that **WAV** is selected.

5. Select **Start** and your song will be exported. After exporting, you'll see that FL Studio has generated a list of files, as shown in the following screenshot:

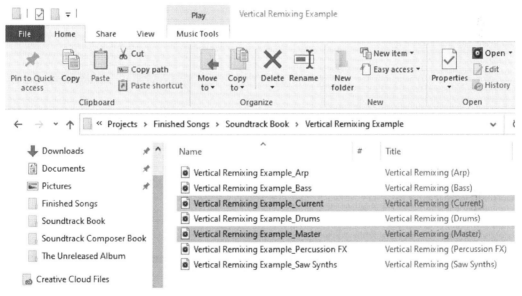

Figure 7.30 – Files generated

Each mixer channel track records audio sent to it and creates a new audio track.

In the preceding screenshot, you'll notice there are highlighted files called **Vertical Remixing Example_Current** and **Vertical Remixing Example_Master**. The **Vertical Remixing Example_Current** file is the song before any effects are applied on the master channel. The **Vertical Remixing Example_Master** track is the song after any effects have been applied on the master channel.

It's good practice to then go and rename each file for later convenience when recombining layers. You'll likely want to include the song tempo and key in the filename.

If you were to drag all the exported audio clips back into FL Studio, you'd see they all line up in sync with one another, as shown in the following screenshot:

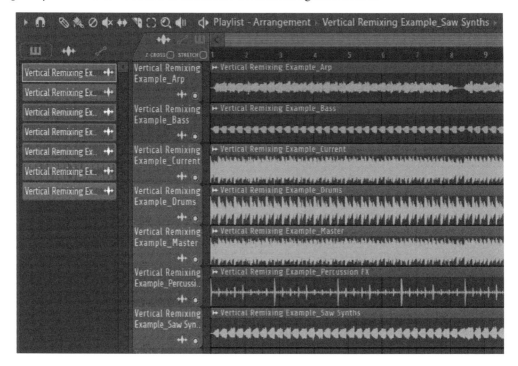

Figure 7.31 – Reimported clips

Notice how all the audio layers line up with each other. They're all in sync and the same length, which is what we need for vertical remixing.

You now know how to create layered music clips to be used in vertical remixing.

Summary

In this chapter, we learned how to create interactive music. Interactive music is music that changes throughout video games depending on events occurring in the game. This creates a much more immersive experience for the player.

We learned about the audio engine middleware Wwise, which is used to set up music in video games. We learned how horizontal re-sequencing can be used to create music that evolves over time, helping to make music less repetitive. We learned how to implement this feature in Wwise.

We learned about vertical remixing to change the instrumentation of a song during gameplay depending on actions occurring in the game. We saw how to implement this in Wwise.

Finally, we learned how to create music for vertical remixing in FL Studio.

In the next chapter, we will learn how to overcome writer's block when composing music. We will introduce a series of templates to ensure that your music is of production-level quality. Finally, we'll discuss resources for additional learning.

8
Soundtrack Composing Templates

We've covered a huge array of topics in this book. Now it's time to make everything efficient and production-ready. In this chapter, we'll learn how to overcome writer's block. We'll then look at a series of templates you can use to ensure your music is production-ready. Finally, we'll discuss resources for continuing your musical adventure beyond this book for further learning.

In this chapter, we'll cover the following topics:

- Overcoming writer's block
- Soundtrack composing template checklists
- Sharing your music
- Resources for further reading
- Conclusion

Overcoming writer's block

Struggling to come up with ideas for songs? Encountering writer's block? Feel like you've used up all your creative juices and there's no more music in you? Don't worry; I've got you covered. Having writer's block is a normal part of composing. It happens when you first start, and it happens to professionals too. But it's okay; you can and will overcome it. You just need to try a few creative tactics.

Fortunately for you, I've compiled a list of strategies you can use to get started making music whenever you're lacking inspiration. Feel free to refer to this whenever you get stuck:

- Improvise music on an instrument or even try a new instrument.

- Play around with your MIDI keyboard or drumpad.

- Experiment with FL Studio's **Scale** feature and try out new scales.

- Lay down a drumbeat.

- Go through the routine. Open the **Digital Audio Workstation** (**DAW**), set up the project, and add the key sections you intend to write. People think accomplishment comes through the cycle *Inspiration -> Motivation -> Action*, however, really the cycle is *Action -> Inspiration -> Motivation -> Action*. Get started and the ball will start rolling.

- Use an existing song as inspiration. Listen to a song on YouTube and figure out the key chords in the DAW. Shift the chords up or down a few keys, make some chord inversions, and adjust the tempo of the song to something slower or faster. Bam! You have a starting point for a song that already sounds good.

- Use a previous song as inspiration. What if you were to add another verse to your last song?

- Identify music themes. Think about a character from a TV show or movie, for example, Darth Vader, Indiana Jones, or Superman. Then think about the key characteristics they have. If there was a soundtrack for that character, what would it sound like?

- Look at a physical image such as of a place – perhaps somewhere you went on vacation, a location in a video game, or a vivid picture in a magazine or online. Then craft your song around making a melody to fit that image.

- Preset scrolling – pick a synth and scroll around the presets. Play a few notes until you find a sound that feels good.

- Sample scrolling – scroll through samples until you find a tune you can build on.

- Design a new sound by choosing a synth and experimenting. Even if no melody comes up, you'll have a cool new instrument ready for next time.

- Pick a track you like and remix it.

- Try using pre-existing MIDI files. Some people say this is cheating, but I disagree. You can't use a MIDI file on its own and expect a finished song, no matter how good the MIDI file is. MIDI files are a wonderful way to spur some chords to get started. Shift the chords up or down a few notes, add some chord inversions, change the tempo a little, and voil•, you already have something ready to work on.

- Collaborate – bounce ideas off a friend.

- Try a new instrument plugin.

- Try experimenting blindly. Under pressure? Nothing sounding good? Getting frustrated? The mind is more creative when it's having fun and relaxed than when it's under stress. Give yourself permission to fail. Failure is a key step in learning. Add random elements together and see what you come up with. Inspiration sometimes strikes when least expected.

- Experiment with new techniques. Check out YouTube tutorials and learn something new.

- Check out a genre you wouldn't normally try and see what you can come up with.

- Build around the vocal. Do you normally compose a song and add the vocal melody later to fit the song? Try it the other way around – record the vocal, and then craft the song around it.

- Begin with the rhythm. It's often a lot easier to come up with a groove and baseline than it is to come up with a melody. And often the melody magically appears once the baseline is going.

- Use a motif. What's a **motif**? It is a short musical idea or fragments of notes. Write a few notes. The full melody will form later.

- Go to a new location. A new location can give you inspiration. Check out music events and meetups near you.

- Listen to a song you like and think about how you might make something like it.

- Record sounds. Pick a location or an object and record its sound; for example, a café, the store, the beach, the park…

- Set a timer and force yourself to work until the timer ends (30-60 minutes should work).

- Write it out. Sketch out your musical idea on paper or a whiteboard with diagrams, arrows, and colors.

- Think up a story to be told through your song. What's the overall message and feeling you'd like to convey?

- Listen to new music. Consider music from another country or language.

- Consider using the Scaler 2 plugin to come up with melodies:

  Scaler 2 is a music theory plugin that helps you build chord progressions. The following screenshot shows Scaler 2:

Figure 8.1 – Scaler 2

Features offered by Scaler 2 include the following:

- Import an existing song: Scaler 2 can identify the chord MIDI notes used in the song so you can use them in your own composition.

- Given a chord, Scaler 2 can come up with suggestions for chords that logically fit next based on the key. It can suggest these based on a genre or an artist's style.

To learn more and get Scaler 2, visit `https://www.pluginboutique.com/product/3-Studio-Tools/93-Music-Theory-Tools/6439-Scaler-2.`

Soundtrack composing templates

I'm a big fan of checklists – ordered lists to ensure you perform all the prerequisite steps. Checklists allow you to make sure you've paid attention to each step, especially those that are easy to overlook. Some steps feel quite small but, if forgotten, can lead to big problems down the road. The book *The Checklist Manifesto*, by *Atul Gawande*, provides compelling arguments for the benefits of using lists to improve your workflow. I highly recommend reading it.

The steps in composing music are a repeated process that you'll go through again and again for each music production project. Music production steps can be broken down into a sequential list. This section will provide you with a series of lists you can adapt and use to ensure you've paid attention to all the important things while composing. For organizational convenience, there are three checklists for three different stages of the music production process.

The following are checklists for collecting the soundtrack requirements, composing music, and mixing music.

Soundtrack requirements checklist

This checklist is designed to handle the business aspects of soundtrack composing. Using this checklist should help you cover many of the important business tasks you can expect to encounter when consulting on music projects for clients:

1. Walk through the project with the client:

    a. If scoring a movie, watch through the movie with the client and take notes on what emotions are desired at each scene requiring music. Create a list of items that require sound effects.

    b. If scoring a video game, ask what intensity and mood are desired in each level. Create a list of items in the game that require sound effects.

        i. Figure out if the music needs to be interactive.

2. Arrange a system of keeping track of the status of music for submission to the client. *Chapter 1, The Business of Composing for Clients*, provides a method using a Soundtrack Planner document.

3. If the client provided temp music for the project visual, go through each of the temp tracks and ask why the client chose them for the scenes. Ask what the user experience goal is of each scene. This will help you avoid getting overly attached to any particular temp track.

4. Send the Soundtrack Planner to the client for approval to make sure you identified all the items that need music and sound effects.

5. If consulting for a client, draft up an invoice itemizing the services you intend to provide:

   a. Identify all expected costs you expect to incur.

   b. Negotiate the budget. Send the invoice to the client and get their approval.

   c. Get their agreement in writing.

6. Save copies of receipts of any expenses you may incur so you can be compensated by the client and/or for business tax expense deductions.

7. If collaborating with other musicians, establish how you plan to share your music when collaborating. Agree beforehand how you'll notify each other regarding changes to the project. *Chapter 1, The Business of Composing for Clients*, suggests using the Splice software for version control management. Do a demo run with any collaborators to ensure you are both on the same page and can share your projects with each other without issue.

8. Discuss with the client how to deliver music. What format should be used, how should it be labeled, and how should sounds be organized for mutual convenience?

9. If you were able to retain the rights to the soundtrack music you created, it's time to register your music to collect royalties:

   a. Locate the organization that collects royalties for your geographic region. For example, in the United States, you would use the **American Society of Composers, Authors, and Publishers (ASCAP)**, **Broadcast Music, Inc. (BMI)**, or the **Society of European Stage Authors and Composers (SESAC)**.

   b. Register your music to collect public performance royalties using your regional collection body, such as **SoundExchange**.

   c. Upload your music to a digital distribution service of your choice to get your music onto streaming platforms to collect royalties. If you choose to use DistroKid as your digital distribution provider service, the following link provides you with a discount on your first year: `https://distrokid.com/vip/seven/701180`.

Composing music checklist

This checklist is designed to handle the composing aspects of music composition. Using this list should help you come up with better-sounding compositions for any song:

1. For each song, go through your requirements (such as set out in the Soundtrack Planner described in *Chapter 1, The Business of Composing for Clients*) and identify the key emotions, intensity, and purpose for your music.

2. Consider identifying music motifs/themes for each character or setting of significance.

3. With your desired emotion in mind, select a music scale to use in your song.

4. Select an appropriate tempo and time signature for your song.

5. Create a chord progression.

6. Select/create instruments that can deliver the sound you want to use. You can reuse these instruments for multiple songs if you save your song projects and presets in an organized manner.

7. Spread and transpose instrument notes up or down so you achieve a nice balance of high and low sounds. If all your notes exist in the same octave, you're likely missing out on a much larger and more pleasant sound that could be achieved by spreading out your notes.

8. Explore ways to add rhythm and movement to your composition. Add vertical note movement and spacing rests to make your melodies more interesting. For example, if your melody movement goes upward, you can have your chords go downward. Done strategically, you can make your melodies sound like they're feeding off each other.

9. Layer your instruments' sounds with other instruments.

10. For each live instrument, add articulations, expression, and velocity to increase the realism and interest of the sound. If your note timings are coming across as too robotic, consider whether to add some randomness to your note timing to mimic the random variation that comes with human playing.

11. Add volume dynamics to your instrument melodies. Add crescendos and decrescendos to fade instruments in and out.

Mixing music checklist

This checklist is designed to handle the mixing and mastering steps for each song you compose. Following this checklist should help you achieve polished music that is production-ready:

1. For each instrument, consider applying compression, saturation/distortion, or other effects to achieve the desired sound.

2. Balance the volumes of each instrument to emphasize your main melody.

3. Identify whether instruments are drowning each other out and use EQ to give space to each instrument. Check for phase interference between instruments.

4. For each instrument, apply subtractive EQ tweaks to remove offensive resonant sounds.

5. Consider adding reverb effects to make your instruments feel like they are being played in the same room to add realism.

6. Master your music. If you don't have mastering software already, I recommend Izotope's Ozone plugin. In the mastering chain, you'll likely want to do the following:

   a. Identify frequency range zones for your song: low, mid, and high frequencies. Most mastering plugins use three or four frequency ranges.

   b. Using a stereo image plugin, improve the stereo width.

   c. Apply EQ to balance out your low and high frequencies.

   d. Add compression to the overall mix.

   e. Use a dynamic equalizer and apply subtractive EQ to your mix.

   f. Add a limiter/maximizer to prevent peaking and increase the overall volume to the desired loudness.

7. Save any complex mixing and/or mastering chains as a preset so you can quickly apply them later on if the client requires adjustments.

   In the FL Studio Mixer, it's very easy to save or copy all the effects on a mixer track to another track. You can save any selected mixer track by going to **Mixer Options | File | Save mixer track state as…**. The following screenshot shows an example:

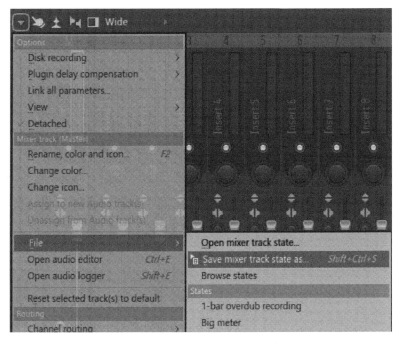

Figure 8.2 – Saving a mixer track

Doing the preceding step can save the preset to a file on your computer, which can be opened up in an entirely different project. Alternatively, you can click the **Save mixer track state as...** button and drag it onto another mixer channel. This will copy the selected mixer track effects onto another track.

8. Submit music to the client and receive feedback/approval frequently. Remind the client to provide feedback or approval after submitting each song. Sending all the songs at the end and hoping that they will like everything is a recipe for disaster.

You may be unfamiliar with some of the terminology discussed in the music mixing checklist. Topics on mixing and mastering go beyond the scope of this book. If you're interested in learning the fine details of mixing and mastering, consider checking out my book *The Music Producer's Ultimate Guide to FL Studio 20*. I also offer courses teaching these topics at `https://www.chestersky.com/`.

Summary

In this chapter, we learned how to overcome writer's block. We also looked at several template checklists you can follow to check you've paid attention to important steps in the music creation process.

Share your music

If you'd like to share your music with other readers and students and ask for feedback from fellow musicians, feel free to post your music in the following Facebook group: `https://www.facebook.com/groups/musicproducerandcomposercommunity`.

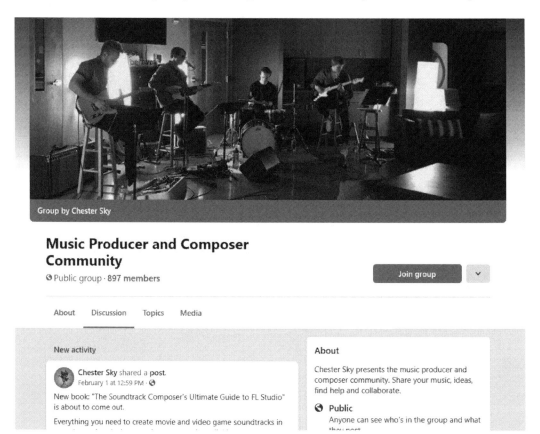

Figure 8.3 – `Facebook` page of the Music Producer and Composer Community

The group is intended to share music and resources for musicians.

Next steps

If you enjoyed reading this book and are wondering what your next steps could be, there are lots more resources available to continue your musical journey.

More from the author

If you'd like to deep dive inside FL Studio and learn about mixing, mastering, and music marketing/publishing, check out my book *The Music Producer's Ultimate Guide To FL Studio 20: Create production-quality music with FL Studio*, by Packt Publishing.

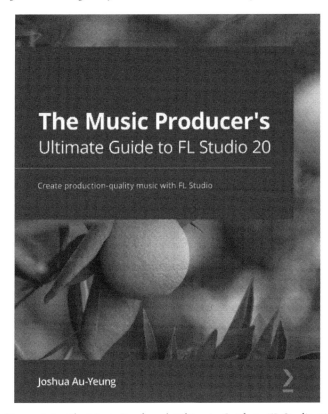

Figure 8.4 – The Music Producer's Ultimate Guide to FL Studio 20

In this book, you'll explore FL Studio's vast array of tools and discover best practices, tips, and tricks for creating music. You'll learn how to set up your studio environment, create beats, compose melodies and chord progressions, mix sounds with effects, and export songs. As you advance, you'll find out how to use tools such as the Piano roll, mixer console, audio envelopes, types of compression, equalizers, vocoders, vocal chops, and tools for increasing stereo width.

The book introduces you to mixing best practices and shows you how to master your songs. Along the way, you'll explore glitch effects and create your own instruments and custom-designed effect chains. You'll also cover ZGameEditor Visualizer, a tool used for creating reactive visuals for your songs. Finally, you'll learn how to register, sell, and promote your music to earn royalties.

Video courses

I offer a variety of bestselling courses on music production, FL Studio, and soundtrack composing. If you're interested in enrolling in my courses or checking out additional products I offer, visit the website `https://www.chestersky.com/`.

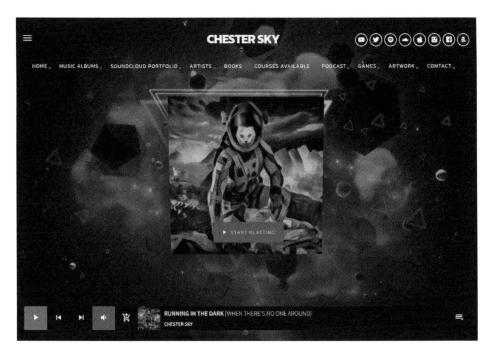

Figure 8.5 – Chestersky.com

On the website, you'll find courses on music production and soundtrack composing.

Social accounts

If you enjoyed this book, feel free to get in touch. I also regularly post music production resources on my social accounts:

- **Website**: `https://www.chestersky.com/`
- **Facebook**: `https://www.facebook.com/RealChesterSky/`
- **Twitter**: `https://twitter.com/RealChesterSky`
- **Instagram**: `https://www.instagram.com/iamchestersky/`

A few final thoughts

There's an unlimited supply of great music to use as inspiration. Pay attention to music in films, games, and songs you like. It's a good habit to try to identify tools and techniques that might have been used in songs.

Try to keep your eye on the big picture and not worry too much about the little problems that show up along the way. Setbacks and uncertainty should be expected. Most skills are hard when new, but they become easier through experience. Projects, clients, and tools come and go. What stays is your ever-improving ability to create slightly better music with each song you work on. Each musical piece you create helps make your next piece even better. What you're able to do now is nothing compared to what you'll be able to do down the road.

Soundtracks are meant to be emotional listening experiences. If your music isn't generating an emotion, you probably need to go back to the drawing board.

Although academics may try to argue otherwise, there's no such thing as perfection in music. Music is an art form. You don't have to be great when you start. You get good through experience. Whether or not other people like your music now is not an indicator of whether you'll make great music in the future. Just focus on making music that sounds good to you and the rest will sort itself out.

Make music you like and care about. You're the composer, so you're in charge.

Remember to enjoy the process. Making music is best when it's fun. Have fun making music!

Conclusion

You've reached the end of the book. I hope you had a fun adventure learning how to compose music. With a little practice, you'll have widely applicable music composition skills to design emotional experiences. You're now fully armed with tools and techniques to compose music for any project you dream up.

Further reading

If you want to learn about the business side of a music career, I highly recommend the book *How to Make It in the New Music Business: Practical Tips on Building a Loyal Following and Making a Living as a Musician*, by *Ari Herstand*. This book is hands down the best book I've read on the music business. I cannot recommend it enough.

In this book, we briefly alluded to services that collect royalties. You may be wondering, how exactly do royalties get collected and what share of royalties do you get? On the surface, this sounds like a simple question. It turns out the legal details are really complex. If you want to learn how royalties are collected, read the book *All You Need to Know about the Music Business*, by *Donald Passman*.

Index

Symbols

12-tone equal temperament
frequency (Hz) 73

A

American Society of Composers, Authors
and Publishers (ASCAP) 27
articulations
reference list 109
string instrument-specific, list 110
using 109-111
Art of Foley 153
audio
rendering, to wave form 170-173
audio stems 63

B

Broadcast Music, Inc. (BMI) 27
Browser tool 54-56

C

CD Baby
URL 29

Channel rack tool
about 38-41
shortcuts 41
Circle of Fifths chord wheel
using 92-96
clients
meeting, preparing for 10, 11
C major scale 80
cognitive dissonance
about 163
example 163, 164
collaborators
digital audio workstations 20-23
music, sharing with 19
composer
toolkit 66
creepy music
about 166, 168
audio, rendering to wave form 170-173
designing 168
detuned 168
effects 176
keys, modifying midway 168
note combinations 176
note combinations, techniques 176-182
playing, backward 169, 170

slowing down 173-175
speed, changing abruptly 173-175
speeding up 173-175

D

Dehumaniser
  about 155
  reference link 155
diegetic music 153, 154
Digital Audio Workstation (DAW) 224
DistroKid
  URL 29
Ditto Music
  URL 29
divisi 119
double stops 119

E

EastWest Sounds
  reference link 101
epic music
  about 188
  composing, for trailers 188-190
equalization (EQ) 129
expression
  adding, manually to orchestral
      instruments 112-115
  adding, with fine-tuned method to
      orchestral instruments 115-118
  need for 112
  using 111

F

fear 162

feeling of tension
  creating, for trailers 188-190
  creating, techniques 188-190
film
  music, composing for 12
  watching, with client 14
FilmFreeway
  Categories 8, 9
  URL 7
FL Studio
  about 34
  audio, recording 56-59
  core tools 35-37
  music, exporting 59-63
  music, for vertical remixing in 215-220
  reference link 35
  trial version 34
  trial version, features 34, 35
FL Studio, core tools
  Browser tool 54-56
  Channel rack 39-41
  Channel rack tool 38
  Mixer 50-53
  Piano roll, using 41-44
  Playlist 45-48
FL Studio project
  sheet music, creating in
      MuseScore from 136-143
freezing audio 170
Fruity Video Player
  about 143
  used, for syncing music to
      visuals 143-147

G

ghost notes
  muting 44

H

happy music
    composing 184, 185
    composing, techniques 184, 185
horizontal re-sequencing
    about 203
    implementing, in Wwise 204-207

I

Igniter
    about 156
    reference link 156
iMusician
    URL 29
interactive music 192, 193
Ionian mode for C 80

J

jump scare
    about 164-166
    designing 164

K

key signature 92
Krotos
    about 155
    reference link 155

L

LANDR
    URL 29
leitmotifs
    about 67, 68
    using 68, 69
live orchestras
    considerations 131
Loudr
    URL 29

M

markers
    about 147
    setting 147-150
mechanical royalties 27
Meetup
    URL 6
MIDI notes sound, creating like
        live string instruments
    tips 126
MIDI programming
    used, for composing
        orchestral music 118
Mixer tool 50-53
modes
    about 79-82
    using 82, 83
modes, usage
    ghost notes for scale reference,
        using 86-90
    notes 83-85
motifs
    about 67
    using 68, 69
    versus themes 68
MuseScore
    about 136
    sheet music, creating from FL
        Studio project 136-143
music
    collaborating, challenges 19, 20

composing, for films 12
composing, for specific moods 183
composing, for video games 12, 13
composing, tips 23-25
networking 6
sharing 232
sharing, with collaborators 19
syncing, visuals with Fruity
    Video Player 143-147
Musical Instrument Digital
    Interface (MIDI) 40
music composer
profession, establishing 5
music composing
experience 7-10
tasks 26, 27
music ideas
researching, for project 18
music jobs 4
music production
resources 233
resources, on social accounts 234
video courses 234
music royalties
collecting 27-29
music score
planning 11
music terminology
sharps and flats 90-92

N

Native Instruments
reference link 101
notes
deleting 44
splitting 45

note velocities
random variation, adding 127, 128

O

octave 71
Omnisphere
about 158, 159
reference link 158, 159
Opus 102
orchestral chord progressions
composing, tips 122-126
orchestral compositions
mixing, considerations 128-130
orchestral instrument plugins
articulations, using 109-111
expression, adding manually to 112-115
expression, adding with fine-
    tuned method to 115-118
expression, need for 112
expression, using 111
paid recommendation 101, 102
recommendation 98-101
significance 102, 103
velocity, using 103-109
orchestral music
composing 98
composing, with MIDI
    programming 118
creating, with orchestral
    instrument plugins 98-101
Orchestrator 102

P

perfect fifth 71
Piano roll
ghost notes, muting 44

notes, deleting 44
notes, splitting 45
using 41-44
Playlist
    about 45-48
    patterns, versus songs 48-50

R

Randomize 178
Randomizer 127
random notes
    generating, steps 178
Record Union
    URL 29
Reformer
    about 157
    reference link 157
rendering to audio 170
reproduction royalties 27
reverb 129
ReverbNation
    URL 29
romantic music
    composing 187, 188
    composing, techniques 187

S

sad music
    composing 185-187
    composing, techniques 185-187
Scaler 2
    reference link 226
scales
    12-tone equal temperament
        frequency (Hz) 73
    about 70-74

need for, composing 74-78
using, for compose 74-78
Western music, using 12 notes 74
scary music
    note combinations 176
    note combinations, techniques 176-182
scary sound
    about 166
    designing 166, 167
    types 166, 167
sheet music
    about 136
    creating, in MuseScore from FL
        Studio project 136-143
Society of European Stage Authors
    and Composers (SESAC) 27
Society of Motion Picture and Television
    Engineers (SMTPE) 146
SoundBetter
    about 10
    URL 9
SoundCloud
    URL 5
sound effects
    about 153
    examples 154
    libraries 159, 160
    plugins 155
    reference link 160
SoundExchange
    about 28
    URL 28
soundtrack
    requirements, gathering for
        design document 14
soundtrack composing templates
    about 227
    music checklist, composing 229

music checklist, mixing 230, 231
   requirements checklist 227, 228
Soundtrack Planner
   about 15
   creating 15-17
Spectrasonic's Omnisphere plugin
   reference link 102
Splice
   about 21, 22
   URL 21
   version control with 20-23
spooky music
   composing 162
string orchestral instruments
   composing 119
   considerations, with vocals 120-122
   divisi 119
   double stops 119
surround mics 131
Symphonic
   URL 29

T

temp music 14
themes
   about 67
   using 68, 69
   versus motifs 68
time signatures
   about 150
   setting 150-152
tonic note 77
tree mics 131
TuneCore
   URL 29

V

velocity
   using 103-109
version control
   with Splice 20-23
vertical remixing
   about 207
   implementing, in Wwise 207-214
   music, creating in FL Studio for 215-220
video games
   about 12
   music, composing for 12, 13

W

Wave Works Interactive Sound
      Engine (Wwise)
   about 194-203
   horizontal re-sequencing,
      implementing in 204-207
   vertical remixing, implementing
      in 207-214
Weaponiser
   about 158
   reference link 158
whole tone 181
wide mics 131
writer's block
   overcoming 224-226

Packt.com

Subscribe to our online digital library for full access to over 7,000 books and videos, as well as industry leading tools to help you plan your personal development and advance your career. For more information, please visit our website.

Why subscribe?

- Spend less time learning and more time coding with practical eBooks and Videos from over 4,000 industry professionals

- Improve your learning with Skill Plans built especially for you

- Get a free eBook or video every month

- Fully searchable for easy access to vital information

- Copy and paste, print, and bookmark content

Did you know that Packt offers eBook versions of every book published, with PDF and ePub files available? You can upgrade to the eBook version at packt.com and as a print book customer, you are entitled to a discount on the eBook copy. Get in touch with us at customercare@packtpub.com for more details.

At www.packt.com, you can also read a collection of free technical articles, sign up for a range of free newsletters, and receive exclusive discounts and offers on Packt books and eBooks.

Other Books You May Enjoy

If you enjoyed this book, you may be interested in these other books by Packt:

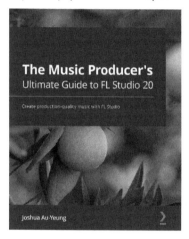

The Music Producer's Ultimate Guide to FL Studio 20

Joshua Au-Yeung

ISBN: 978-1-80056-532-6

- Get up and running with FL Studio 20
- Record live instruments and vocals and process them
- Compose melodies and chord progressions on the Piano roll
- Discover mixing techniques and apply effects to your tracks
- Explore best practices to produce music like a professional

Jumpstart Logic Pro 10.6

Jay Asher

ISBN: 978-1-80056-277-6

- Get to grips with Audio and MIDI and how they are different, along with covering Apple Loops

- Record and edit audio, such as your voice or guitar

- Create and edit MIDI parts, using Logic Pro's software instruments

- Develop realistic drums and electronic drums with Logic Pro 10.5's amazing Drummer

- Explore the new Step Sequencer, Live Loops, and Quick Sampler that were included with version 10.5

Packt is searching for authors like you

If you're interested in becoming an author for Packt, please visit `authors.packtpub.com` and apply today. We have worked with thousands of developers and tech professionals, just like you, to help them share their insight with the global tech community. You can make a general application, apply for a specific hot topic that we are recruiting an author for, or submit your own idea.

Share Your Thoughts

Now you've finished *Music for Film and Game Soundtracks with FL Studio*, we'd love to hear your thoughts! Scan the QR code below to go straight to the Amazon review page for this book and share your feedback or leave a review on the site that you purchased it from.

https://www.amazon.in/review/create-review/error?asin=%3C180323329X%3E

Your review is important to us and the tech community and will help us make sure we're delivering excellent quality content.

Made in the USA
Middletown, DE
02 March 2023

26056583R00148